AMAZING STORIES

OTTAWA SENATORS
Great Stories From The
NHL's First Dynasty

HOCKEY
by Chris Robinson

PUBLISHED BY ALTITUDE PUBLISHING CANADA LTD.
1500 Railway Avenue, Canmore, Alberta T1W 1P6
www.altitudepublishing.com
1-800-957-6888

Copyright 2004 © Chris Robinson
All rights reserved
First published 2004

Extreme care has been taken to ensure that all information presented in
this book is accurate and up to date. Neither the author nor the
publisher can be held responsible for any errors.

Publisher	Stephen Hutchings
Associate Publisher	Kara Turner
Editors	Stephen Smith, Debbie Elicksen, Gayl Veinotte

We acknowledge the financial support of the Government
of Canada through the Book Publishing Industry Development
Program (BPIDP) for our publishing activities.

Altitude GreenTree Program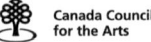
Altitude Publishing will plant twice as many trees as were used
in the manufacturing of this product.

We acknowledge the support of the Canada Council for the Arts which
in 2003 invested $21.7 million in writing and publishing throughout Canada.

Canada Council   Conseil des Arts
for the Arts   du Canada

National Library of Canada Cataloguing in Publication Data

Robinson, Chris, 1967-
   Ottawa Senators / Chris Robinson.

(Amazing stories)
Includes bibliographical references.
ISBN 1-55153-790-7

   1. Ottawa Senators (Hockey team)--History. I. Title. II. Series: Amazing stories
(Canmore, Alta.)

GV848.O89R62 2004   796.962'64'0971384   C2004-903744-7

An application for the trademark for Amazing Stories™
has been made and the registered trademark is pending.

Printed and bound in Canada by Friesens
2 4 6 8 9 7 5 3

Comments on other *Amazing Stories* from readers & reviewers

"*Tightly written volumes filled with lots of wit and humour about famous and infamous Canadians.*"
Eric Shackleton, *The Globe and Mail*

"*The heightened sense of drama and intrigue, combined with a good dose of human interest is what sets* Amazing Stories *apart.*"
Pamela Klaffke, *Calgary Herald*

"*This is popular history as it should be... For this price, buy two and give one to a friend.*"
Terry Cook, a reader from Ottawa, on **Rebel Women**

"*Glasner creates the moment of the explosion itself in graphic detail...she builds detail upon gruesome detail to create a convincingly authentic picture.*"
Peggy McKinnon, *The Sunday Herald*, on **The Halifax Explosion**

"*It was wonderful...I found I could not put it down. I was sorry when it was completed.*"
Dorothy F. from Manitoba on **Marie-Anne Lagimodière**

"*Stories are rich in description, and bristle with a clever, stylish realness.*"
Mark Weber, *Central Alberta Advisor*, on **Ghost Town Stories II**

"*A compelling read. Bertin...has selected only the most intriguing tales, which she narrates with a wealth of detail.*"
Joyce Glasner, *New Brunswick Reader*, on **Strange Events**

"*The resulting book is one readers will want to share with all the women in their lives.*"
Lynn Martel, *Rocky Mountain Outlook*, on **Women Explorers**

AMAZING STORIES

OTTAWA SENATORS

To my grandfather Roy Robinson — who passed away just before I started writing this book — and to my uncle Bart Robinson... both, unfortunately, Toronto Maple Leaf fans.

Contents

Prologue 11
Chapter 1 The Capital of Hockey 13
Chapter 2 The NHL's First Dynasty 21
Chapter 3 Bring Back the Senators 31
Chapter 4 The Shot Heard Around Ottawa 47
Chapter 5 The Tale of Two Captains 57
Chapter 6 On the Brink... 74
Chapter 7 Battle of Ontario 92
Epilogue 124
Bibliography 126

Prologue

Ottawa, May 23, 2003. Conference Final. Game Seven

Despite season-long ownership, payroll, and bankruptcy troubles, the Ottawa Senators are one game, one goal, away from reaching the Stanley Cup finals for the first time since 1927. They have rallied from a 3-1 game deficit against the mighty New Jersey Devils to even the series at 3-3.

The Senators head into the third period down 2-1. Less than two minutes into the period, an Ottawa defenceman poke checks the puck away from Devils' forward Jeff Friesen. Ottawa's Marian Hossa grabs the puck near centre and skates into the New Jersey zone. He spots Radek Bonk on the left side and passes. Bonk takes the feed and blasts the puck past Devils goalie, Martin Brodeur. The crowd explodes. The building shakes. The score is 2-2.

Inspired by Bonk's goal, along with the deafening roar of 18,500 fans, the Senators take the play to the Devils. They come close to taking the lead, but can't beat Brodeur.

With just over three minutes to go, the game remains tied. The Corel Centre is filled with a level of tension and anticipation that it has never experienced before. It looks like the game will go into sudden-death overtime.

Ottawa Senators

All of a sudden, Devils' forward Jeff Friesen dumps the puck towards the left side of centre ice. Winger Grant Marshall collects it at centre and skates towards the Senators zone. As Marshall races down the left side of the Senators zone, both Ottawa defencemen converge on him. What they don't realize is that Friesen is now wide open and heading towards the Senators goal. Marshall quickly fires the puck over to Friesen. Defenceman Wade Redden, realizing his mistake, races back to check Friesen before the puck reaches him. But as he turns, he stumbles slightly and the puck passes him. Friesen collects it. He dekes to the left on the Senators goalie, and shoots the puck....

Chapter 1
The Capital of Hockey

Ottawa was not the birthplace of hockey, but from the early 1880s until the late 1920s it was certainly its capital. Not only was Ottawa home to hockey's first dynasty, the Ottawa "Silver Seven," it was also the birthplace of the Stanley Cup.

Between 1891 and 1902, hockey fever seized the nation's capital. Hockey teams, sponsored by local businesses, began playing throughout the city. Both senior and junior teams sprang up all over the region. Some of the prominent early teams included the Rideau Rebels, the Ottawa Electrics, Enright's Boarders, The Bronsons, the Ottawa University team, and, most famously, the Ottawa City Hockey Club (later known as the Silver Seven).

Ottawa Senators

The Rideau Rebels were one of the city's earliest teams. Their origin is unique. In 1888, Lord Stanley of Preston arrived from England to serve as Canada's governor general. His three sons were such big fans of hockey, Stanley built a rink for them on the grounds of Rideau Hall. Initially, the rink was used for casual games between members of Stanley's household, but in 1889, two of his sons, Algernon and Arthur, decided to form a competitive team. By 1891, the Rebels challenged the Ottawa City Hockey Club for the national championship.

During the early 1890s, the Rebels toured across Ontario to promote hockey. Lord Stanley watched many of these games and developed a fondness for the sport. Just before Stanley returned home to England in early 1892, he drafted a letter for his colleague, Lord Kilcoursie (who was also a member of the Rebels) to read at a gathering of the Ottawa Amateur Athletic Club. The contents of that letter, published in *The Ottawa Citizen*, would change the face of hockey.

"I have for some time past been thinking that it would be a good thing if there were a challenge cup which should be held from year to year by the champion hockey team in the dominion.

"There does not appear to be any such outward and visible sign of championship at present, and considering the general interest which the matches now elicit, and the importance of having the game played

The Capital of Hockey

fairly and under rules generally recognized, I am willing to give a cup which shall be held from year to year by the winning team.

"I am not quite certain that the present regulations governing the arrangement of matches give entire satisfaction, and it would be worth considering whether they could not be arranged so that each team would play once at home and once at the place where their opponents hail from."

The reading of the letter was greeted with hearty applause. Kilcoursie then announced that he had been asked to place an order for the cup.

Created in England, the Stanley Cup took less than a month to make. The Cup featured a sterling silver bowl with a gold-plated lining mounted on an ebony block. It cost $50.

Before the Stanley Cup became the exclusive property of the National Hockey League in 1926, teams from professional and amateur leagues across Canada challenged for it. Cup holders often faced as many as five challenges per season.

The most prominent Ottawa team of this period — and the first to challenge for the Stanley Cup — was the Ottawa City Hockey Club. Initially nicknamed the Ottawa Capitals, they competed for the hardware in 1894 and 1897, losing to the Montreal AAA and Montreal Victorias respectively. During the Cup's first 10 years, Montreal teams (AAA, Shamrocks, and Victorias) would also dominate.

Ottawa Senators

Ottawa would finally bring home its first Stanley Cup in 1903. The team's rise that year coincided with the arrival of a rookie named Frank McGee. Although McGee would only play four seasons with Ottawa before retiring at age 24, in that short time, he became hockey's first superstar by leading the team to four straight Stanley Cup championships (including nine Cup challenge defences during that time). What made McGee's accomplishments all the more impressive was that he was partially blind in one eye.

During a charity game for the families of Boer War veterans, McGee — who was playing for the Canadian Pacific Railway team — was struck in the eye by a puck. Despite his injury, McGee continued to play hockey. He was only 5'6" and 140 pounds, but McGee overcame his small size with deft skating and scoring skills. As Hall of Fame player Frank Patrick (who played against McGee) said, "He had everything — speed, stickhandling, scoring ability, and was a punishing checker. He was strongly built but beautifully proportioned and he had an almost animal rhythm."

McGee's statistics were astounding. In the 23 games he played for Ottawa from 1902 to 1906, McGee scored 71 goals (assists weren't recorded). That's an average of over three per game. In 22 playoff games, McGee scored 63 times. Those are numbers even the great Wayne Gretzky would admire.

During his short stint with the Silver Seven (they had gained the nickname for their Stanley Cup success), McGee — who played the now extinct seventh position of rover —

The Capital of Hockey

was complemented by a talented group of players, including the high-scoring Gilmour Brothers (Dave, Bill, and Suddy), Harry "Rat" Westwick, pointman Arthur Moore, and goalie Bouse Hutton. The Silver Seven were captained by Harvey "the Bytown Slugger" Pulford, a tough-as-nails defensive defenceman. Like all great teams, Ottawa could beat the opposition at any game. They were a highly skilled team that weren't afraid to rough it up.

In what was one of the most exciting Stanley Cup games ever, the Silver Seven's remarkable reign (along with the career of Frank McGee) came to an end in March 1906 in a two-game, total-goal series against their regular league rivals, the Montreal Wanderers. Both teams finished the season with identical 9-1 records. Their only losses came against each other.

Game one took place in Montreal on March 14, 1906. After the Wanderers kept the Silver Seven off the scoreboard during an early three-minute man advantage, Montreal struck for three goals in less than eight minutes. Ottawa continued to attack, but they looked like an old and tired hockey team. Just before the half, a Harvey Pulford penalty led to a Montreal goal. At halftime, the Wanderers had a 4-0 lead.

Ottawa started strong in the second half, but a save on Harry Smith by Wanderers goalie, Henri Menard, seemed to crush their momentum. The Wanderers scored five more times in the second to win 9-1.

Ottawa was in shock. *The Ottawa Citizen*'s headline the

following day read: STANLEY CUP HOLDERS MET WITH DISASTER. The article went on to say, "The Ottawas were completely outplayed by the Wanderers at all stages of the game."

More than 5400 fans jammed into a rink that was equipped for 2000 to 3000 people.

Ottawa fans clearly believed the Silver Seven could come back in game two.

The Silver Seven didn't let them down. After the Wanderers took a 1-0 lead 12 minutes into the game, McGee made it 1-1 on a rink-long rush. A goal by Harry Smith and a second by McGee put Ottawa up 3-1 at halftime.

Heading into the second, the Wanderers' series lead was 10-4. Ottawa quickly cut the lead in half when Harry Smith, Alf Smith, and Rat Westwick scored in quick succession. Harry Smith then scored two more goals to bring the Silver Seven to within one goal of the Wanderers, with 10 minutes to play.

Ottawa tied the game on a bizarre play. Harry Smith went down after taking a vicious crosscheck from a Wanderers player. Smith then slid, with the puck underneath him, into the Wanderers net. The goal counted. The series was tied at 10-10.

"The scene in the arena was simply astounding," reported *The Citizen*, "and the cheering that shook the vast structure (after the Silver Seven's ninth goal) lasted many minutes, while the huge tiers and banks of people were gesticulating humanity."

The Capital of Hockey

Harry Smith scored again, but the play was ruled offside. The rink erupted, according to *The Citizen*, "with a terrific storm of hoots and jeers."

With less than two minutes remaining, the Ottawa defencemen were caught pinching in the Wanderers zone. Lester Patrick of the Wanderers flipped the loose puck past the Ottawa defenders towards forward Moose Johnson, who sped in alone on the Ottawa goal. As Johnson came towards the Ottawa net, he left a drop pass for Patrick who fired it past Ottawa netminder Percy LeSueur. With 90 seconds left, the Wanderers had an 11-10 lead in the series. Just before the final bell, Patrick scored again to make give the Wanderers a 12-10 series victory.

The Silver Seven's incredible comeback had fallen short. Their remarkable four-year reign — which saw them defend the title 10 times — as Stanley Cup champions came to a memorable but disappointing end.

During the off-season, Frank McGee (only 24 years old) retired to take a steady job with the Canadian government. Despite his impaired vision, McGee later volunteered to fight during World War I. He was wounded in battle in 1915, but chose to return to action in France. He was killed during the Somme offensive at Courcelette on September 16, 1916. Like many, his body was never found.

The day after the game, *The Ottawa Citizen* featured a front-page cartoon showing a Montreal player hoisting the Cup. The caption beneath the cartoon read: "Say *Au Revoir*,

Ottawa Senators

but not Goodbye."

The caption proved prophetic. The Ottawa Senators would bring the Cup back to Ottawa in 1909 and 1911 before going on to become the first dynasty of the newly formed National Hockey League.

Chapter 2
The NHL's First Dynasty

hile World War I raged on in Europe in 1917, the Ottawa Senators (along with the Montreal Canadiens, Montreal Wanderers, and Toronto Arenas) were becoming a charter member of the newly formed National Hockey League (NHL).

The move turned out to be a good one for the Senators. During the NHL's first decade, they finished first seven times and won four Stanley Cups on their way to becoming the league's first dynasty. What made their achievements all the more inspiring was the assortment of adversities that the team faced.

The NHL was founded for a relatively simple and immature reason: spite. The National Hockey Association (NHA)

Ottawa Senators

owners had grown tired of the antics of Toronto Shamrocks owner Eddie Livingstone. For years, Livingstone had been fighting with the league over a variety of scheduling, player, and ownership issues. However, the NHA realized that they could not simply toss Livingstone out of the league without facing a lawsuit. Instead, the other NHA owners simply decided to walk away from the NHA and form a new league without Livingstone. On November 26, 1917, in Montreal's Windsor Hotel, they did just that by formally creating the new National Hockey League.

At this time, three men owned the Ottawa Senators: Martin Rosenthal, Edwin (Ted) P. Dey, and Tommy Gorman. Rosenthal's involvement with the team dated back to 1901. When the struggling franchise tried to withdraw from the NHA in 1916, the request was rejected, and the team was turned over to Dey — who ran the city's Dey Arena. Gorman (who was also *The Ottawa Citizen*'s sports editor) became involved just prior to the creation of the NHL. Through friends, Gorman learned that the Senators were folding and that the entire franchise (including players) was available for $5,000. Gorman borrowed $2,500 and bought into the team, with Rosenthal and Dey putting up the remainder of the money.

After missing the playoffs in their inaugural season, the Senators — led by forwards Punch Broadbent, Frank Nighbor, Cy Denneny, and Jack Darragh, along with defensive star Sprague Cleghorn and goalie Clint Benedict —

The NHL's First Dynasty

quickly established themselves as a dominant force in their second season, finishing in first place. However, the Senators stumbled in the playoffs, losing 4-1 to the Montreal Canadiens in the NHL finals.

Their success from 1918 to 1919 was all the more remarkable given that the team faced a pre-season tragedy when forward Hamby Smith died of influenza at age 32. At the end of the season, the Senators played an exhibition game to raise money for Smith's gravestone.

During their first Cup victory in 1920 over the Seattle Millionaires, the weather was so bad that the players were, literally, skating in slush. With no hope of getting suitable ice conditions in Ottawa, NHL president Frank Calder decided that the remainder of the series would be moved to the artificial ice at Toronto's Arena Gardens. Ottawa fans were heartbroken, but with the teams sometimes playing in over an inch of water, the NHL had no choice but to find a better venue.

After Seattle won game four to even the series, Senators' star Jack Darragh (normally a mild-mannered fellow) was so frustrated that he threw his skates down and said, "I've had enough hockey for this winter. You will have to get along without me in the final game." He then hailed a taxi to Union Station and took the first train home to Ottawa.

After arriving in Ottawa, Darragh was convinced to take the first train back to Toronto.

It's a good thing he did. With the teams tied 1-1 after two

periods, Darragh exploded for three goals to lead the Senators to a 6-1 blowout of the Metropolitans and their first Stanley Cup in almost a decade.

The first game of the 1923 NHL finals is described by Ottawa historian Bill Galloway as "one of the wildest, dirtiest hockey games ever played in a Cup series." There was bad blood right from the start. The Canadiens came at the Senators hard, attempting to punch, kick, elbow, and injure any Ottawa player who got in their way. The Senators, however, were no pushovers. By the second period, the Canadiens were already wearing down because of their aggressive play. After Cy Denneny scored in the third to give the Senators a 2-0 lead, the Canadiens, frustrated by their inability to crack their opponent's zone, finally snapped. As Denneny scored, Canadiens' defenceman Billy Couture slugged the Senators forward. Denneny collapsed to the ice with blood streaming from his head.

With Denneny gone and the Canadiens forced to play shorthanded for the remainder of the game after Couture was ejected, it was the fans' turn to snap. They began throwing bottles, papers, and whatever else they could get their hands on at the referees and the Ottawa players. The game had to be stopped twice to clear the debris from the ice. Finally one of the referees grabbed a megaphone and asked the crowd to stop. They responded by throwing fruit and the game had to be interrupted several more times.

In the dying minutes of the game, former Senator

The NHL's First Dynasty

Sprague Cleghorn went to work. After Senators' rookie Lionel Hitchman bodychecked Cleghorn's brother, Odie, Sprague raced to his aid and attempted to crosscheck the rookie. Hitchman, however, saw Cleghorn coming and belted him with a bodycheck that sent the Canadien to the ice.

Two minutes later, as Hitchman wound up to take a shot, Cleghorn charged over and knocked Hitchman to the ice with a hard blow to the head. As Hitchman slumped to the ice, Cleghorn continued to jab at him. The referees eventually interceded and tossed Cleghorn from the game. Seeing their Stanley Cup hopes dashed, the Montreal fans became angrier. When the final bell rang, one fan rushed at referee Lou Marsh and struck him in the face. Marsh returned the favour and knocked the assailant down. He then fled to the safety of his dressing room.

The crowd immediately turned its attention to the Ottawa Senators. Backed against their bench, the Ottawa players started swinging their sticks in defence. Montreal police finally broke in to fight off the crowd and the Senators escaped, barricading themselves in their dressing room. It took police another half hour to disperse the Montreal mob.

Before the NHL had a chance to step in, Canadiens' manager Leo Dandurand suspended Couture and Cleghorn prior to game two in Ottawa.

The Canadiens won a significantly cleaner game two by a score of 2-1. However, the Senators won the series three goals to two and moved on to the Stanley Cup finals where

Ottawa Senators

they defeated the Vancouver Maroons three games to one.

Following the win over Vancouver, the Senators went on to defeat the Western Hockey League champion Edmonton Eskimos by scores of 2-1 and 1-0 to win their third Stanley Cup in four years.

The Eskimos series was best remembered for the bizarre turn of events in the final game. Having already subbed in on defence, centre, and both wings, the Senators' young defenceman, King Clancy, was called upon to guard the nets when goalie Clint Benedict was assessed a minor penalty (goalies had to serve penalties in those days). That night, Clancy — who didn't allow a goal — became the only player in NHL history to play every position. Given modern rules (goalies no longer have to serve their own penalties) and the addition of back-up goalies, Clancy's record is unlikely to be duplicated.

Following the 1923-24 season, Gorman and Dey found a new ownership partner in Frank Ahearn. The Ahearns — who owned Ottawa Electric and the Ottawa Electric Streetcar Line — were one of Ottawa's wealthiest families. Not long after, Gorman and Ahearn bought out Dey. Soon, Ahearn and Gorman built a new home for the Senators: the 10,000-seat artificial ice arena called The Auditorium.

Despite the retirement of team captain Eddie Gerard and the ineffectiveness of Jack Darragh (who was convinced to return to the Senators for the 1923-24 season), the Senators continued to tear up the NHL, this time finishing

The NHL's First Dynasty

with a league leading 16-8 record. However, they were beaten 1-0 and 4-2 by the Montreal Canadiens in the NHL finals.

After the season, Jack Darragh retired once and for all. During his 13-year career with the Senators, the Ottawa-born winger won four Stanley Cups and averaged over a point per game.

Sadly, Darragh didn't have a chance to change his mind about retirement. That summer he suffered a ruptured appendix and died. He was only 34 years old. Darragh's hockey achievements would not go unnoticed. In 1962, he was inducted into the Hockey Hall of Fame.

In 1924, expansion fever hit the four-team NHL. They added the Montreal Maroons and Boston Bruins to the league and increased the schedule to 30 games. In order to help the new franchises, each existing team was asked to part with two players. Ottawa sold the Maroons Punch Broadbent and Clint Benedict. The Senators could afford the loss of their two veteran stars. Broadbent's play had slipped considerably during the past two seasons, and the Senators had an up-and-coming goaltender named Alex Connell ready to replace Benedict.

Aside from the addition of Connell, the Senators added four new players: defencemen Alex Smith and Ed Gorman, and right-wingers Reginald "Hooley" Smith (whose early season play impressed the team so much that they sold Lionel Hitchman to Boston) and local boy Frank "Shawville Express" Finnigan.

Ottawa Senators

The new additions, especially Gorman and Hooley Smith, played well, but they couldn't prevent the Senators from stumbling to a fourth place finish, and for the first time since the NHL began, out of the playoffs.

NHL expansion continued in 1925. The Pittsburgh Pirates and New York Americans (who inherited the Hamilton Tigers' entire roster after the Tigers players went on strike for more playoff pay in 1924-25) paid $15,000 to join the NHL. Only four years earlier, the Montreal Canadiens had sold for just $4,000.

That same year, Tommy Gorman took full advantage of the rising value of franchises and sold his share in the Senators to Frank Ahearn for $35,000.

The Senators made only one roster change before the 1925-26 season, adding an 18-year-old left-winger with blazing speed named Hec Kilrea. The Senators rebounded from their sub-par season in 1924-25 and finished in first place with a record of 24-8-4. But once again, they faltered in the NHL finals. This time, the Senators lost a close two-game, total-goal series, 2-1.

After the season, the Pacific Coast Hockey Association and Western Canada Hockey League — which had merged to form the Western Hockey League — folded completely. The Stanley Cup now became the exclusive property of the NHL.

Prior to the 1926-27 season, the NHL expanded to 10 teams. The league was divided into an American and Canadian division. The schedule was increased to 44 games.

The NHL's First Dynasty

With a record of 30-10-4, the Senators, once again, finished atop the NHL standings. In the Canadian division final, the Senators eliminated the Montreal Canadiens and then defeated the Boston Bruins in the NHL finals to win the Stanley Cup for the fourth time in eight years. It would be the last time the Ottawa Senators held the honour.

Off the ice, the franchise was in trouble. During their Cup-winning season, the team lost $50,000. Skyrocketing player salaries and a decrease in attendance hurt the Senators. With fewer than 30,000 people, the city of Ottawa simply could not compete with the larger cities. In order to stay afloat, the Senators were forced to sell off their assets. Between 1927 and 1930, Hooley Smith, Ed Gorman, Cy Denneny, George Boucher, Punch Broadbent (who had returned to the Senators in 1927-28), and Frank Nighbor were all sent to other teams.

Following the economic crash of 1929 and the onset of the Depression (not to mention a dismal 10-win season in 1930-31), Ahearn (who was now more interested in a political career than hockey) suspended operations for the 1931-32 season. Frank Finnigan and King Clancy were loaned to the Maple Leafs. Finnigan returned to Ottawa when the Senators resumed play in 1932-33, but Clancy remained in Toronto.

The Senators continued to sink, finishing last in 1932-33 and 1933-34.

In 1934-35, the Senators moved the franchise to St. Louis. The only player remaining from the 1927 championship was

Ottawa Senators

Frank Finnigan. The St. Louis Eagles finished in last place, winning only 11 of 48 games. Before the season was done, the Eagles sold Finnigan to the Maple Leafs, where he remained until 1937. The Eagles folded after their inaugural season. It was a sad and bitter end for hockey's greatest franchise.

The Ottawa Senators were dead, but their accomplishments remained. No other team would come close to matching their success until the Toronto Maple Leafs won five Stanley Cups in the 1940s.

Chapter 3
Bring Back The Senators

"Bruce Firestone is nuts and local fans are being led through the petunia patch if Bruce Firestone really thinks he can land an NHL expansion franchise for Ottawa this century, well into the next, or ever."
Alan Eagleson, Executive Director, the National Hockey League Player's Association, September 8, 1989.

hen real estate developer Bruce Firestone of Terrace Investments announced, in June 1989, his intention to bring an NHL team back to Ottawa, everyone thought he was crazy. The mayor told him that Ottawa was just a civil-service town with too small a market to entice the National Hockey League. Besides, Toronto and Montreal already had a huge fan base in

Ottawa and would never allow a team here. Even Firestone's father, renowned Ottawa businessman, civil servant, and art collector, Jack Firestone, had doubts about his son's plans. "I wouldn't do it, but God bless him."

The criticism didn't stop Firestone, who was seen as a bit of oddity in the business world — he was laughed at when he once proposed turning a downtown bank into a casino. But he was a man who never took no for an answer. Firestone firmly believed that Ottawa had matured into a world-class city. He argued that the private business sector had exploded in Ottawa, attracting thousands of small companies to the area. Furthermore, Ottawa was a hockey hotbed with a long and rich history. Most importantly, Firestone maintained that they had money. "The NHL will take us seriously because we have a bunch of money to wave in their faces."

Firestone first thought about the possibility of landing an NHL franchise in 1987 while jogging along the Ottawa River Parkway. He knew that the NHL was talking about expanding and thought to himself, "Why not Ottawa?" Given Ottawa's hockey history and the fact that it was the capital of the very country that "owned" hockey, it made perfect sense that the city should have a professional hockey team.

Firestone fine-tuned the idea for a year before finally sharing it with a couple of Terrace employees (Cyril Leeder and Randy Sexton) after, appropriately enough, a game of pick-up hockey. Usually very wealthy individuals bought sports franchises, but Firestone, whose wealth was not quite

Bring Back the Senators

that deep, had an alternative. In theory, the plan was simple. Terrace would buy up 600 acres of land located in the middle of nowhere at a cheap price. Once the franchise was approved, they would build a $100-million arena on 98.5 acres of the land. This would drive up the value of the surrounding 500 acres. Firestone eventually dreamed of the area becoming a mini-city for 9,000 people called West Terrace. If it worked, Terrace's net worth would jump from its current $105 million to $400 million by 1997. In order for this to happen, Terrace would need to find about $138 million to buy the franchise and pay for the arena. Secondly, they'd need to have the agricultural land rezoned so that they could use the site for commercial purposes.

Sexton and Leeder reacted with surprise. In fact, Leeder, who had studied sports franchises, thought the idea was ridiculous. But Firestone pressed on and eventually convinced both the young, aspiring businessmen to help him prepare a bid to bring an NHL team to Ottawa.

On June 12, 1989, Firestone sent a letter to NHL president John Ziegler stating Terrace Investments' intent to seek an expansion franchise. Ten days later, Terrace held a local press conference announcing plans to build a $55 million 20,000-seat arena along with a $30-million hotel, retail, and office complex on a site west of the city, near Kanata. The money would all come from Terrace Investments' $100 million in assets. Firestone asked local citizens to show their support by sending in a non-refundable commitment of $25 for season ticket reservations. Firestone knew that he needed to show the NHL that Ottawa fans were serious about supporting a team.

Terrace put on a good show, but how much credibility was there to the application? Some felt that Firestone was using the bid as a way to pass new zoning laws that would help future Terrace development projects. And where would this $100 million come from? In 1987, Terrace's assets were valued at $7 million.

Terrace also faced stiff competition outside the city. At least 10 other North American cities including Milwaukee, Houston, Seattle, Hamilton, Anaheim, Tampa, Phoenix, Miami, San Diego, and St. Petersburg, were said to be vying for expansion spots.

Terrace didn't even have a name for the team. They had planned on using "Senators" but immediately faced two lawsuits: one from the Gorman family who owned the rights to the name, the other from a junior hockey team with the same name.

Factor in the very loud voices of doubt from all circles and it wasn't surprising that ticket sales were slow. Clearly, the people of Ottawa had their own doubts about the validity of Firestone's dream.

None of these obstacles slowed Firestone down. By September 1989, Terrace managed to secure the rights to the Senators name and held a news conference announcing the start of a "Bring Back The Senators" campaign. The highlight of the conference was the introduction of Frank Finnigan, the last surviving member of the Ottawa Senators' 1927 Stanley Cup championship team.

In December 1989, the NHL officially announced that it would add seven expansion teams by 2000. The entry fee was set at US$50 million, an astonishingly high figure given that 14 of the NHL's 21 franchises were not even worth that much with players. Although Firestone had anticipated a fee of no more than US$35 million, he didn't blink at the $50-million fee — at least publicly. The first teams to be accepted would be announced in December 1990. Firestone was convinced Ottawa would be one of them.

Throughout 1990, Firestone and Terrace worked day and night to keep their bid moving along. They wined and dined the NHL owners (and even sent them birthday cards), produced colourful publications, brought in the NHL's most successful coach, Scotty Bowman to advise them, and received approval from the Ottawa region to build on land in Kanata.

In August, they produced an extraordinary, leather-bound, 600-page application package. The application was then delivered by limousine to the NHL's head offices in New York. In all, Terrace spent over $3 million on the bid.

The people were starting to believe. By the summer of 1990, over 11,000 season ticket reservations had been received. The Ottawa mayor changed his tune and began actively supporting the bid. The franchise received additional good news when it learned Ontario's Liberal government was in support of their rezoning application. Still more good news arrived when leading contender, Milwaukee, withdrew its application.

Meanwhile, many in the media still believed that Ottawa had no chance of getting a franchise in an NHL that was moving away from family-owned towards corporate-run teams. With players' salaries rising, did Ottawa have any hope of competing with the big boys? Firestone's wealth paled in comparison to the deep pockets in Toronto, Detroit, and New York. Besides, how would adding Ottawa help the NHL get a lucrative U.S. television deal?

As the Terrace delegates headed to Florida in December 1990 for the expansion announcement, they were cautiously optimistic. About 150 very loud supporters accompanied Terrace to the sunshine state, including a marching band that paraded up and down the street in front of the main hotel. Terrace built a miniature hockey rink in their hotel suite and almost everywhere you turned, there was an enthusiastic Senators supporter with a "Bring Back the Senators" t-shirt. If franchises were awarded based on enthusiasm, then Ottawa was a runaway winner.

During the meetings, Firestone gave an emotional and impressive 45-minute presentation to the owners. The presentation was well-received and everything seemed to be going according to plan until an NHL governor approached the Ottawa table at dinner and told them they had no chance of winning. Firestone and his crew were devastated.

On December 6, the Ottawa group waited in a backroom as the NHL board convened to make their decisions. Firestone was convinced they had lost their bid. Finally, at 1 p.m., he was summoned and escorted down a fire escape and through a kitchen. Firestone figured he was being led to a room where he would watch the winners being announced with representatives from the other losing bids. Finally he was shown into a meeting room with the group from Tampa Bay. When they entered the room, the NHL governors stood up and started congratulating them. Firestone didn't grasp what was happening until he glanced down at an NHL press release announcing that Ottawa and Tampa Bay had been approved as new NHL franchises. Firestone burst into tears. Two years of hard work in the face of many pessimists had paid off. Ottawa was back in the NHL.

NHL executives praised Terrace's professionalism. "If you're assessing how these guys have handled expansion, they should publish a textbook on it," noted Vancouver Canucks' operations director Brian Burke. "If anyone told you 12 months ago their chances were better than zero, they were lying. What they've done is amazing."

"At first we thought it was a pipe dream," said Edmonton Oilers' owner Peter Pocklington. "They kept at it for two years, barraging us with information on how good it was and finally, they showed us some real numbers."

In the end, though, Firestone was right. It came down to

cold, hard cash. The biggest reason Tampa Bay and Ottawa got approval was that they never questioned the franchise fee nor did they request (unlike, for example, Hamilton) changes to the fee payment schedules.

The City of Ottawa was overwhelmed. People celebrated in the streets. Ottawa was in the big leagues.

The celebrations were short-lived. There was still a lot of work to be done before the Senators' home opener in October 1992. Not only did the franchise need a manager, coaches, scouts, and players, they also needed to raise some money. The Ottawa media remained skeptical. Who were Firestone's other backers? Some commentators feared that Ottawa taxpayers would be saddled with the costs of a new arena if Firestone couldn't come up with the money, much as Toronto taxpayers had covered the costs of the city's SkyDome Stadium.

The franchise itself was conditional. Each successful applicant had to make three payments to the NHL: $5 million within 10 days of receiving the franchise; $22.5 million in June 1991; and $22.5 million in December 2001.

By January 2, 1991, less than a month after they'd been awarded the franchise, the Senators' first season — which was played in the 10,000-seat Ottawa Civic Centre — was sold out. On January 14, Firestone made the first fee payment of US$5 million.

Terrace was now actively seeking investors in order to meet its second and third payment obligations. But the economy had sunk into a recession and investors were hesitant to

Bring Back the Senators

support the Senators until a ruling on the land zoning had been made. Publicly Firestone told people not to worry, that he had numerous investors, but it soon became apparent that this was not the case. By March 1991, the lack of investment in the Senators was a hot topic across the country.

This wasn't the franchise's only problem. The issue of rezoning for the site of the future arena was again in question when the New Democratic Party (NDP) defeated the Liberal government. The NDP were not supportive of the Senators' rezoning classification. Firestone would have to convince the Ontario Municipal Board that their proposed new home for the Senators was not going to be built on prime farmland.

Nineteen ninety-one proved to be a challenging year for Firestone. Unable to afford experienced hockey professionals, Firestone — who was quickly drifting into a background role — let the inexperienced Randy Sexton and Jim Durrell (who was also the mayor of Ottawa) run the team. From the start, both men were out of their league. Durrell, in particular, was a questionable choice. When Durrell continued to serve as mayor, local citizens became furious over the potential conflict of interest. Durrell (who eventually resigned as mayor in February 1991) also annoyed the NHL by starting a rumour that the Senators might be ready to join the league for the 1991-92 season, an absurd statement given that the team had no hockey personnel in place. Word quickly spread around league circles that the Senators were incompetent and unprofessional.

Ottawa Senators

The Senators' second payment of $22.5 million was due on June 3. How would Firestone be able to come up with the money in three months? Investors wouldn't bite until there were assurances about the land. It was a catch-22. The land zoning hearings wouldn't begin until May and a ruling wouldn't likely be made until August. Even the NHL began to show signs of concern. They insisted that the Senators place the $14 million from ticket sales in trust in case fans had to be reimbursed should the franchise be rescinded.

In early May, a ray of hope emerged when entertainer Paul Anka, an Ottawa native, was introduced as the Senators' second biggest investor. The Senators felt that Anka's involvement would give them instant international credibility and help them attract more investors. Anka spoke of the joy he felt returning home and helping out his hometown. According to the terms of the deal, Anka would receive just over half a million dollars worth of units in the team. He would also have an option to buy half the Palladium Arena for $4 million. (On February 27, 1996, the Palladium was renamed the Corel Centre after the Senators struck a 20-year deal with an Ottawa-based software company.) Anka was also to receive $450,000 for three concerts. He would be named an alternate governor, serve on the team's advisory board, and receive a $50,000 annual salary. The team would also create a Paul Anka Award, to be given to the player most dedicated to the team and community. In exchange, Anka would bring in $10-million worth of investors. The deal was a

Bring Back the Senators

good one for Anka and clearly the Senators were desperate. They'd promise the moon if they could.

In late May, the Ontario Municipal Board (OMB) hearings began. Things were going so poorly during the proceeding that Firestone, against the advice of his partners, made a concession not to develop anything on the land but the Palladium Arena for 25 years.

Meanwhile, the June 3 payment deadline came and went with both Tampa Bay and Ottawa failing to send their fees. The Senators, thanks in large part to a bank loan taken out against the season ticket money they had in trust, managed to make the payment two weeks late on June 15.

Things weren't all bad for the Senators. They landed television and radio deals, negotiated a pouring rights deal with Molson, and managed to do relatively well with merchandise sales. But it wasn't enough to keep Firestone from a long and anxious summer as he awaited word from the OMB.

The OMB ruling finally came down at the end of August. They voted in favour of the rezoning, but with conditions: Terrace would have to spend an extra $20 million dollars on the cost of a highway overpass; the stadium would have be scaled down from 22,500 seats to 18,500; and the number of luxury boxes reduced from 176 to 104. It didn't matter. Firestone was ecstatic. Against all odds, Firestone had won yet again.

After the ruling, investors didn't exactly bang down the doors, but the job of selling the Ottawa Senators became a little easier, especially when Ottawa entrepreneur Rod Bryden entered the picture. Bryden was approached by a desperate Firestone to help secure financing. Bryden agreed and through the investment firm Wood Gundy managed to raise about $20 million. But this was still short of the $22.5 million needed for the December payment. On December 16 — deadline day — Bryden put in the remaining money from his own pocket. In exchange, he was given a 50 per cent share of Terrace and became the new C.E.O. of the Ottawa Senators. The Senators made their final payment to the NHL, and on December 21, 1991, they became an unconditional NHL franchise. Now they just needed players.

Securing the players, not suprisingly, was just as difficult for the Senators as securing the money had been. While teams were busy sending scouts to various international tournaments throughout 1991, the Senators didn't hire their first hockey employee until after the OMB ruling. In August they introduced former NHL player Mel Bridgman as the new general manager of the Senators. The Senators had hoped to land former Edmonton Oiler manager John Muckler, but he tired of waiting for an offer and instead signed with Buffalo. Desperate, the Senators turned to Bridgman, who had no hockey management experience. In truth, he was probably all they could afford.

Bridgman had his work cut out for him. The Senators did not have a single scout and they were already months behind the other teams when Bridgman took over in

Bring Back the Senators

September. Bridgman didn't help his case when he hired six inexperienced scouts. Ironically — given the league's current abundance of European talent — the Senators biggest shortcoming was in Europe. No one on staff was overly familiar with the European leagues. Bridgman called former Winnipeg Jet manager John Ferguson — who was considered one of the pioneers of European scouting — to see if he would be interested in becoming the Senators' director of player personnel. Ferguson accepted the offer and began preparing for the upcoming draft.

But first the club laid the groundwork for the expansion draft. The Senators and Tampa Bay Lightning were allowed to pick players made available from the other NHL teams. The draft was a bit of a joke. Each team was allowed to protect two goalies and 14 players. First- and second-year players were not eligible and no team could lose more than one goalie, one defenceman, or two forwards. Any team that lost a goalie in the last expansion draft was exempt from making another one available. Teams could also make trades until the last minute to protect more players. In the end, there was little in the way of immediate help available. The few veteran players who were left unprotected came with salaries too rich for the Senators. The remaining crop consisted mostly of American Hockey League-calibre players.

Expansion draft day turned in a comedy of errors for the Senators. When they entered the draft room, they discovered their computer — which held all their draft information —

had broken down. With NHL executives and coaches present, and with hockey fans across Canada watching the procedure on television, the Senators began an embarrassing selection process. Relying solely on printed lists, each decision took longer. NHL president John Ziegler and vice-president Brian O'Neill grew increasingly irritated as cameras continued to run, while the disorganized Senators scrambled through their printed lists. The Senators were lost without the computer. No one seemed able to keep track of the choices without it. First, the Senators went up to select Montreal's Todd Ewan. But they were told that Montreal could not lose any more players. The Senators returned to their table and mulled over the next possibility. They returned and picked Todd Hawkins from the Maple Leafs. Again, they were told that the Leafs — who had lost two players to Tampa Bay — could not lose any more players. Finally, the Senators hit rock bottom when they picked C.J. Young, a player who wasn't even on the final list. Ziegler sent the Senators table an angry note telling them to get their act together. Eventually they did and when the day was done, the Senators had 21 players including veterans Peter Sidorkiewicz, Mike Peluso, Mark Lamb, and Laurie Boschman.

The entry draft, held a few weeks later, went somewhat better. They had originally hoped to get talented Czech defenceman Roman Hamrlik, but when Tampa Bay beat them to it they selected a dazzling forward from Russia named Alexei Yashin.

Bring Back the Senators

The Senators, for better or worse, now had a team.

Under the guidance of coach Rick Bowness, who was hired after the Boston Bruins let him go, the Ottawa Senators prepared for their inaugural season. Fans and media were realistic. The Senators would not be a very good team. They followed a "play now, pay later" philosophy. They simply did not have the money to go out and sign any big name players. The club would rely on character and toughness. The Senators might lose a lot of games, but it wouldn't be for a lack of effort. If fans were patient, the team would be competitive around year five. The people of Ottawa were dizzy with excitement as season one approached. Most didn't care if the team was bad. They were just proud that, after a 58-year absence, hockey had finally returned to Canada's capital. They could live through the growing pains.

Ottawa's opening game on October 8, 1992 was, fittingly, against the Montreal Canadiens at home. The atmosphere was electrifying. A noisy sold-out crowd of 10,449 crammed into the intimate Civic Centre (which would serve as the Senators' home until the opening of the Corel Centre in January 1996).

As the lights dimmed, the Civic Centre shook with anticipation. The spotlight fell on a gladiator, whose trumpet blared the Senators' new theme song. Roman columns — each lit from within — descended onto the ice before dancing gladiators in white emerged and performed a dance routine. As they finished, Canadian figure skating champion

Ottawa Senators

Brian Orser was introduced.

The supremely kitsch routines went on far too long. Ottawans had already been saddled with the Ice Capades for decades. They wanted to see NHL hockey not figure skating.

The lights remained dim as the team's song thundered through the building. One by one, the new Ottawa Senators were announced. Each player received enormous applause. The loudest cheers were saved for goaltender, Peter Sidorkiewicz, slick scoring Sylvain Turgeon, and tough guy Mike Peluso. All three would satisfy their fans on this evening.

With the Senators at centre ice, the nine Stanley Cup banners were raised to the roof, alongside Frank Finnigan's retired #8 jersey. When Bruce Firestone appeared to say a few words about Finnigan, he was greeted with a raucous chant of "Bruce, Bruce, Bruce!" Firestone looked pleased but dazed as he introduced Frank Finnigan Jr., along with former Finnigan teammate, Ray Kinsella. The arena shook again as the fans roared their approval for the rising banners.

The arena was so small you could hear individual voices. At one point, a happy voice screamed, "WE WANT THE CUP!"

Forty-five minutes after the lights first dimmed, and after a rousing, infectious rendition of the national anthem by local pop star Alanis Morrisette, the puck was finally dropped on Ottawa's first NHL game since 1933.

Chapter 4
The Shot Heard Around Ottawa

There wasn't much to like about the Ottawa Senators following the 1995-96 season. For the fourth consecutive year, they finished at the bottom of the NHL standings. During the season, they went through two general managers, three coaches, and another contract dispute with star forward Alexei Yashin.

However, there was, if not quite a silver, at least a bronze lining. General manager Randy Sexton (who had replaced Mel Bridgman) was fired mid-season and replaced with the Senators' first experienced hockey man, Pierre Gauthier. Gauthier worked fast to turn things around. He signed holdout Yashin to a five-year deal, fired interim head coach Dave Allison (who had replaced Rick Bowness only 22 games earlier) and replaced him with former St. Louis Blues coach Jacques Martin. Gauthier then swung a three-way deal with the New York Islanders and Toronto Maple Leafs that saw the Senators acquire goalie Damian Rhodes and highly touted defenceman Wade Redden. In a matter of weeks, the Senators became a significantly improved organization.

The timing couldn't have been better. On January 17, 1996, the Senators finally began to play in their luxurious new 18,500-seat arena. Before a raucous sold-out crowd, the club defeated the Montreal Canadiens 3-0.

The team still finished the season with a league-worst 41 points, but it was their best season yet.

Training camp for 1996-97 opened with more optimism than usual. "When general manager Pierre Gauthier brought in Jacques Martin and a new staff, it was a real change in direction," Senators' defenceman Steve Duchesne said. "We all knew that things could turn around. There was a reason to believe."

During the summer of 1996 (highlighted by Daniel Alfredsson winning the Calder Trophy as the NHL's best rookie), Gauthier gave the Senators a much needed facelift, bringing in veterans like Ron Tugnutt, Shaun MacEachern, Shawn Van Allen, and Jason York, along with youngsters Wade Redden, Andreas Dackell, and Sergei Zholtok. Only 18 of the 50 players from the start of the previous season remained. The new additions gave the Senators more depth and strength in goal and on defence, along with more speed at forward.

The Shot Heard Around Ottawa

Daniel Alfredsson with the Calder Trophy

The pressure was on the Senators as they opened the season. Their expansion cousins from Tampa Bay had already made the playoffs with the same ownership and staff they started with in 1991. The Senators, meanwhile, had changed owners, management, coaches, the entire public relations staff, and every single player from the 1992 roster. It was time for the Senators to step forward and play meaningful hockey.

The season got off to a relatively good start when the Senators came back three times to earn a 3-3 tie with the Montreal Canadiens. Damian Rhodes provided solid goaltending, and Wade Redden made an impressive debut by collecting his first NHL goal and earning the game's third star. Up front, Alexandre Daigle played with new energy, consistently using his speed to drive to the net.

By the first quarter mark of the season, the Senators had earned 18 points in 20 games. They were in 10th place in their conference, two spots back of a playoff spot. If they kept up the pace, they'd hit the 74-point mark, a 33-point increase over last year. But would it be enough to make the playoffs? The previous year, the New Jersey Devils had collected 86 points and still missed the playoffs.

Despite the improvements, the Senators still had their share of problems. They weren't scoring enough goals, and the team lacked a single, strong leader whose presence alone could inspire. Yashin was in a scoring slump, and Daigle, after a strong start, seemed lost without injured linemate Radek Bonk.

By the halfway point of the season, their hopes for a playoff spot seemed slim. After 41 games, their record was 12-21-8. The team was tied for 12th place in the conference, four spots back of a playoff spot. To earn a playoff berth, the team would likely have to earn 50 points in their remaining 42 games. It was a tall order for a team that had finished December with four wins in 12 games.

Off the ice, the Senators were also having problems. Despite playing in one of the finest arenas in the world, there were many empty seats. In February, owner Rod Bryden

The Shot Heard Around Ottawa

began the first of his many threats to move the team, telling the city that if people didn't start supporting the Senators, they were going to lose the team.

The Senators' slim hopes of a playoff berth deteriorated at the beginning of March when they dropped four games in a row — including three during a California road trip. With only 16 games remaining, there were four teams between the Senators and the final playoff spot. The slump prompted *Ottawa Citizen* columnist Roy MacGregor to pronounce, "It's over and to a man they know it." Besides, the Senators had already achieved more than was expected of them. That the team was still in the playoff hunt while playing without their two best defensive defencemen in Sean Hill and Stanislav Neckar and #1 goalie Damian Rhodes — all lost to season-ending injuries — was itself a sign of progress.

Apparently, the Senators didn't hear MacGregor's ominous pronouncement. After the disastrous California trip, the Senators lost only two of their remaining nine games in March. Heading into the final month of the season, the team was suddenly within a point of the final Eastern playoff spot.

Taking heed of Bryden's threat, Ottawa fans packed the Corel Centre as the team marched towards the playoffs. Since Bryden's cry for more support, attendance averaged 18,000 during the last eight home games.

The Senators boosted their playoff hopes in April, thanks to consecutive shutouts by Ron Tugnutt against the Buffalo Sabres and Washington Capitals. The wins gave

Ottawa Senators

Ottawa 71 points. They had a two-point lead over the Hartford Whalers and a three-point lead over the Washington Capitals. But losses to Pittsburgh and Philadelphia on April 5 and 6 saw that lead vanish and Hartford vaulted ahead of Ottawa into eighth place.

On April 9, Hartford and Ottawa met in what was, at that moment, the most important game in franchise history. A win would still leave the Senators tied with Hartford. A loss would almost certainly put an end to their playoff dreams.

The city was caught up in playoff fever. All day long people were talking about the Senators. Just months earlier, you'd be hard pressed to find a taker for complimentary tickets to a Senators–Whalers match, but now a ticket to see two sub-.500 teams was the hottest ticket in town.

As the teams hit the ice, the Corel Centre shook. "We felt it from the beginning, from the anthems on," described Senators' captain Randy Cunneyworth. "The emotion, the vibes flowing freely. We had chills down our spines during the anthems and that was a big factor in our start."

And what a start it was. Just 1:52 into the game, Steve Duchesne (who had begged Ottawa management not to deal him at the March trade deadline) fired home a pass from Sergei Zholtok — who had just stripped the puck from a Hartford Whaler — to give the Senators an early 1-0 lead.

Duchesne's goal lifted the team. Andreas Dackell — who hadn't scored in 19 games — put the Senators up by two when he pushed home a Denny Lambert rebound with just

The Shot Heard Around Ottawa

over five minutes remaining in the period. By the end of the first, Ottawa had fired 18 shots at Hartford goalie Sean Burke.

A shorthanded goal by Shawn McEachern gave Ottawa a comfortable 3-0 lead before the game was even halfway through. But a minute later, Hartford's Geoff Sanderson scored to narrow the Senators lead to 3-1.

A power play goal by Andrew Cassels, early in the third period, had the Whalers right back in the game. But less than two minutes later, Bruce Gardiner restored Ottawa's two-goal lead when he parked himself near the Hartford crease and fired home a pass from Alexei Yashin.

Hartford refused to go away, though. Just under three minutes later, Steven Rice picked up a loose puck in the Ottawa crease and flipped it just under Ron Tugnutt's shoulder. Less than a minute later, Cassels stunned the Ottawa crowd when he redirected a Sanderson shot past Tugnutt to tie the game at 4-4.

To their credit, the Senators remained calm. They continued to force the play and generate lots of chances in front of Sean Burke. With just over seven minutes remaining in the game, Hartford's Kevin Haller was called for holding. A minute into the power play, Whalers winger Keith Primeau attempted to clear the puck along the left boards, but Duchesne was there to intercept it. Duchesne skated in, drew a defender to the ice, and then fed Randy Cunneyworth in the slot. Cunneyworth sent a shot between Burke's pads.

A desperate Whaler team, unable to break through the

Ottawa Senators

Senators' defence, tried to create a power play by asking to have Cunneyworth's stick examined. The stick proved to be legal and the Whalers ended up with a delay-of-game penalty.

Shorthanded, Keith Primeau had a chance to score with 1:29 remaining, but Tugnutt made a stunning glove save to preserve the Senators' victory.

A 3-2 win over the Detroit Red Wings two nights later, combined with Hartford's 6-4 loss to the Islanders, put the Senators one point up on Tampa Bay and two points up on the Whalers for the final playoff spot, with one game remaining.

Everyone knew the Senators would be a better team this year, but no one really believed that they had a chance to make the playoffs just yet. Now, they had exceeded all expectations and found themselves one victory away from their first playoff berth since 1930.

Only the stingy Buffalo Sabres and their goaltender Dominik Hasek — arguably the greatest goaltender in the world — stood between the Senators and the playoffs.

With 18,500 screaming fans behind them, the Senators hit the ice for yet another "most important game in franchise history."

As expected, the game was a tight checking–goaltending duel between Tugnutt and Hasek. Outstanding saves by both goalies kept the game scoreless heading into the third period.

Tugnutt, in particular, was sharp in the first period, stopping a number of clear chances, including two break-

The Shot Heard Around Ottawa

aways. He also made a dazzling glove save on a Derek Plante shot, along with two pad saves on Jason Dawe and Rob Ray.

With 36 seconds remaining in the second, Tugnutt made his finest save of the night when he stuck out the left pad to deny Dawe on a clear breakaway.

Hasek stopped all 16 Ottawa shots through two periods. He had to be particularly sharp in the third as the desperate Senators fired 18 shots at him. With 12 minutes remaining, Hasek stopped Alexandre Daigle on a partial breakaway. With 5:48 to go, he got his left arm on a point shot from Janne Laukkanen, and a minute later, Hasek made two brilliant back-to-back saves off Radek Bonk.

Hasek seemed impossible to beat. It was certain the game was heading for overtime.

Then, with less than five minutes remaining, Alexei Yashin carried the puck into the Sabres zone. Fighting off Alexei Zhitnik as he circled around the left faceoff circle, Yashin heard Steve Duchesne screaming for the puck. Taking the pass near the right faceoff circle, Duchesne wristed a low shot past Hasek.

The Corel Centre erupted. The building shook. It was bedlam.

For the final five minutes of the game, 18,500 fans stood and cheered. Then they screamed together as the countdown began: "FIVE! ... FOUR! ... THREE! ... TWO! ... ONE!"

Tugnutt jumped at the final buzzer before being mobbed by his teammates.

Ottawa Senators

Before the Senators headed to their dressing room, the entire team skated around the ice in acknowledgment of their long-suffering fans.

In the dressing room, Duchesne, who admitted that he "was kind of praying on the bench" during the final two minutes, planted a kiss on the cheek of Alexei Yashin, who set up the goal. Other players were shaking like kids at Christmas. The entire city was giddy with joy. After years of suffering watching the Senators and Ottawa Rough Riders (in the Canadian Football League) stumble their way through years of losing seasons, the city finally had a team to be proud of.

The Senators finished in seventh position, meaning they'd be facing the Buffalo Sabres yet again. Despite the Senators' regular season success against the Sabres, Buffalo was heavily favoured to win the series. However, the Cinderella team defied all expectations by taking the Sabres to overtime in game seven before losing on a heartbreaking goal by Buffalo's Derek Plante.

It didn't matter. No one expected a Stanley Cup just yet.

Chapter 5
The Tale of Two Captains

I*t's funny how things work out. Alexei Yashin was the Senators' first player. He was meant to be the franchise saviour. Daniel Alfredsson was just another body, a low draft choice that gave the franchise depth. In the end, it was Alfredsson, not Yashin, who became the franchise leader.

If Yashin's impatience, immaturity, and unprofessionalism mirrored the confounded state of the Ottawa Senators franchise from 1992 to 1997, then Alfredsson's maturity, patience, generosity, and team-first attitude have come to epitomize the entire Ottawa Senators organization since 1997.

When Yashin first donned a Senators jersey for the 1993-94 season, he fulfilled all expectations by leading the team in scoring: 30 goals and 79 points. In fact, he accounted for almost 40 per cent of the Senators goals that year. Yashin was the only rookie selected to play at the NHL all-star game and proved his worth by scoring two goals including the game-winner. Although he helped the Senators improve by 14 points in the standings and finished second in rookie scoring, Yashin was, quite surprisingly, not even a finalist for the Calder Trophy. It didn't really matter, though. After a single season, Yashin was everything Ottawa fans had hoped he'd be: a dominating player who would soon lead the Senators from mediocrity to glory.

The love affair was brief.

Just months after signing Yashin to a five-year, $4-million deal — the most lucrative contract given to any of the 1992 draftees (including first pick Roman Hamrlik) — the Senators gave their other franchise player, 1993 first round choice Alexandre Daigle, an incredible five-year deal worth $12 million. Daigle's contract sent shockwaves throughout the league. How could the Senators pay so much money for an unproven player?

Daigle was young, handsome, and gifted. More importantly, the Senators felt that he was the bilingual cornerstone that the franchise needed to attract both fans and marketing opportunities. However, the contract quickly became a curse on both the Senators and the NHL. Future first round picks would now point to Daigle's contract as the bar. League managers were not happy, and the deal eventually triggered the

The Tale of Two Captains

rookie salary cap that was brought in as part of the new collective bargaining agreement following the 1994 lockout.

Early in the 1993-94 season, Yashin's agent, Mark Gandler, said that despite Daigle's lucrative deal, they had no regrets about their contract. By the end of the season Gandler and Yashin's tune had changed dramatically. "He should be paid much more than Daigle," said Gandler.

Certainly Gandler had a point. Yashin was clearly the best player on the team and he finished almost 30 points ahead of Daigle in scoring. But the Senators refused to budge. "Alexei earned in excess of $1 million (CDN) last season," said Senators owner Rod Bryden. "He earned more than the three finalists for the rookie-of-the-year award. For his agent to request a renegotiation is just not fair."

With each passing week, the war of words escalated. First, Gandler publicly blamed the Senators for their handling of a rookie-of-the-year promotional video, which treated both Daigle and Yashin as equally deserving candidates. "I think Yashin lost the award in the front office. If the team does not think there is a clear choice between Alexei and Alex, why would the writers think it?" Gandler then came forward and said that Sexton had promised to renegotiate Yashin's contract after the first year. The Senators, naturally, denied ever making such a promise. From that moment on Yashin felt betrayed and his relationship with Ottawa slowly headed downhill.

By August of 1994, there was talk of Yashin not attend-

Ottawa Senators

Alexei Yashin

ing training camp and perhaps even demanding a trade. Meanwhile, the Senators faced another contract problem when their 1994 first-round draft pick, Radek Bonk, refused to sign until he received a contract on a par with Daigle's.

While NHL managers didn't exactly admire Yashin and Gandler, they had little sympathy for the Senators predicament. Senators' management had created this mess by giving Daigle such a ridiculous contract. The situation fuelled the existing feeling throughout the league that the Senators were a bush-league operation run by inexperienced hockey people.

Few were surprised when Daigle turned out to be a

The Tale of Two Captains

spectacular bust. During his four and half years in Ottawa, Daigle infuriated fans and management with his apathetic play and late night party habits. He was eventually traded to the Philadelphia Flyers in 1998.

Because of the NHL lockout, the first half of the 1994-95 season was cancelled. The Yashin dispute was not resolved until play resumed in January 1995. The Senators added bonus clauses to his current deal and agreed to renegotiate if he scored 46 points in the shortened 48-game season.

Yashin registered 44 points in 47 games and the Senators refused to renegotiate. "It's very clear in Alexei's contract he had to achieve 46 points," Sexton reported. "It's crystal clear he didn't. We didn't raise the bar on him. He got 44 points, plus we gave him .9 points for the game he missed (benched for mediocre play), so he's at 44.9. You can't get a percentage of a point so he was still two points short."

Yashin and Gandler were furious and demanded a trade. This time Ottawa fans and media were a little more sympathetic towards Yashin's plight. He had clearly established himself as the Senators' franchise player. He was surrounded by mediocre players and still managed to produce all-star type numbers. If the Senators had any hope of becoming a better hockey team, they needed Alexei Yashin.

Yashin's subsequent 177-day holdout would turn out to be the turning point in the franchise and cost many people their jobs. First, player personnel director John Ferguson stated publicly that he sided with Yashin. After Bryden told him to keep his opinions to himself, Ferguson resigned, as did scout Tim Higgins. Without Yashin, the Senators struggled. After only 19 games, coach Rick Bowness was fired (he was replaced by Dave Allison) and on December 10, 1995 Randy Sexton — the man who arguably created the whole mess — was fired as general manager. With the team getting ready to move into their new arena in January of 1996, Rod Bryden (who was not entirely blameless) had clearly tired of the circus that had become the Ottawa Senators.

When the dust had cleared, the Senators were a significantly better organization. Bryden hired experienced hockey man Pierre Gauthier as the new general manager. By the end of the month, Gauthier signed Yashin to a new deal that paid him about $13 million over four years. Yashin was satisfied, for now.

The loss of Yashin during the first half of the season was slightly tempered by the emergence of a 23-year-old Swedish forward named Daniel Alfredsson. Alfredsson, who had spent the previous two seasons playing in the Swedish Elite league, decided he was ready to give the NHL a try. "I had no (NHL) expectations. I'd never even played in a World Junior. I had no thoughts of being drafted," remarked Alfredsson. When the Senators drafted him in 1994, he was stunned.

When Alfredsson arrived at the 1995-96 training camp, he was just another face. In fact, he didn't even warrant a biography in the Senators' media guide. But in a matter of weeks, Alfredsson began writing his own story when he flour-

The Tale of Two Captains

ished during the exhibition season and cracked the Senators roster. After just 19 games, the young Swede was the Senators' best player, leading the team in scoring with 19 points and fuelling early talk about a possible Calder Trophy.

Alfredsson slumped under the brief reign of coach Dave Allison, but by mid-season — now under his third coach, Jacques Martin — he was back on his game and represented the Senators at the NHL all-star game. The new Senators coach was instantly impressed with Alfredsson. "He's a tremendous player and has so many dimensions," Martin observed. "He has the ability to score, but also is extremely good defensively."

Alfredsson appeared to be everything Yashin was not: a responsible, hard working, team player. While Yashin often seemed to be floating, just waiting for a crack to open, Alfredsson was constantly in motion, whether he had the puck or not. And despite his small frame (5'11"), Alfredsson didn't hesitate to go into the corners to dig out a puck.

Even with Yashin back in the lineup, the Senators continued to struggle in the 1995-96 season, once again finishing with the league's worst record. Alfredsson was among the few bright spots of a dismal season. He finished with an impressive 28 goals and 61 points and took home the Senators' first major award when he won the Calder Trophy in June 1996 as the NHL's top rookie.

Led by Yashin and Alfredsson, the Senators quickly jumped from basement dweller to playoff contender in 1996-

97. Alfredsson proved he was no flash in the pan, finishing just four points behind Yashin for the team scoring lead with 24 goals and 71 points in 76 games. It was during the 1997 and 1998 playoffs, in particular, that Daniel Alfredsson really began to emerge as the leader of the Senators.

During the team's first modern playoff series in 1996-97, Alfredsson gave a dominating performance against the Buffalo Sabres, scoring a number of key goals, including an overtime winner. At the beginning of the series, Alfredsson wasn't even on the Sabres map. But by the end, he was all they could talk about.

In game five, Alfredsson seemed to be able to take the puck and do with it as he pleased. It was almost like he was daring the Sabres to come and take the puck from him. When they did, his quick twists and turns left the Sabres reeling.

While Alfredsson was quickly earning respect across the league, Yashin continued to be viewed as a selfish player who cared more about individual than team statistics. Even when Alfredsson held out for a better contract at the beginning of the 1997-98 season, there were few people who didn't sympathize with the Swede's cause. He was one of the lowest paid Senators at the time.

Between 1997 and 1999, Yashin managed only 15 points in 22 playoffs games. His uninspired play led critics to call him the "invisible man." Statistically, the comparison was unjustified. Alfredsson had only managed 19 points during the same period. But it wasn't so much the stats that bothered

The Tale of Two Captains

fans (and teammates) as it was Yashin's apparent lack of effort. Unlike the feisty Alfredsson, Yashin didn't seem to play with any heart. He looked like he had a million better places to be.

Yashin attempted to mend his image. In March 1998, he donated $1 million to Canada's National Arts Centre in the hopes that they might showcase more Russian culture. For a short time, all was forgiven. Yashin was once again the town hero.

Despite his brief holdout at the beginning of the 1997-98 season, Alfredsson returned to help lead the Senators back into the playoffs. The team squeaked into the eighth and final playoff spot and took on the powerful New Jersey Devils in the first round. The Senators weren't given much of a chance against the Devils, but thanks the play of Alfredsson, Yashin, and especially goaltender Damian Rhodes, the Senators took a 2-1 series lead going into the pivotal game four. A win would put them up 3-1. Lose and the series was tied and more importantly, the veteran Devils would get their confidence back.

New Jersey did a decent job of containing Alfredsson in the first three games. He had many scoring chances and was a presence all over the ice, but he hadn't scored a goal. Heading into game four, Devils' coach Jacques Lemaire was adamant the Devils had to contain Alfredsson if they were going to have any success. "Alfredsson has a lot of finesse and quick movements," Lemaire observed. "He is a guy we have to control on the ice. He gives us a tough time. "Unfortunately for Lemaire, the Devils didn't come close to containing Alfredsson in game four. Alfredsson exploded for his most dominating playoff performance to date, scoring three goals and leading the Senators to a 4-3 victory over the Devils.

With or without the puck, Alfredsson's speed challenged the Devils' older and slower defencemen. When they weren't backpedalling each time Alfredsson got the puck in the neutral zone, they gave the puck away to avoid his ferocious forechecking.

Alfredsson's breakthrough performance provided the Senators with a commanding 3-1 lead and they eventually knocked off the Devils 4-2 to win their first modern playoff series. The Senators would lose in the second round against the Washington Capitals, but not before Alfredsson gave another standout performance, netting a hat trick in a 4-3 victory over the Capitals in game two of the series.

It wasn't just Alfredsson's on-ice play that impressed fans and media. During interviews, he was calm, intelligent, and honest. He spoke with a confidence, energy, and enthusiasm that reflected his deep love of the game. Alfredsson was a young man who seemed to be having the time of his life, savouring each and every moment of his career.

That's not to say that Alfredsson didn't have his stumbles — literally. During the 1997-98 season, he missed 27 games, 6 to the contract holdout and 21 to injuries. When he did play, he was flat. As the Senators raced towards a playoff spot in February and March, Alfredsson went into an

The Tale of Two Captains

11-game scoring slump. Alfredsson's 1998-99 season wasn't much better. He tore ligaments in his left knee three days into training camp.

Every time Alfredsson seemed to be on the verge of becoming an NHL superstar, he suffered another injury. Fans started to complain about Alfredsson's wounds and a few even suggested that he be traded. After missing only six games in his first two seasons, Alfredsson missed 71 games between 1997 and 2000. Some wondered if his new contract had taken some of the bite and desire out of his game. That was nonsense, of course. There was no harder working Senator than Daniel Alfredsson. But his game relied on energy, and when you're in and out of the line-up, it's hard to find a rhythm while you're regaining your strength. Alfredsson was as frustrated as everyone else. He was a competitive person who put himself under a lot of pressure. "The expectations for me are a lot higher coming from me than from any media guy or fan."

During 1998-99, Yashin continued to make improvements. He was named the Senators' new captain in October 1998. By mid-season, Ottawa was among the NHL's top teams and Yashin was fifth in league scoring. Yashin, perhaps bolstered by the confidence the organization had shown in him, had finally emerged, it seemed, as a legitimate NHL superstar.

The fairy tale, though, was short-lived.

In January 1999, the National Arts Centre announced

that Yashin had withdrawn the remaining $800,000 left on his donation. At the time, neither Yashin nor the National Arts Centre offered any reason for the withdrawal. Eventually it came to light that Yashin's donation hinged on a secret deal, in which a company run by his parents, named Tatiana Entertainment (named after Yashin's mother), was to be paid $85,000 annually in exchange for the star's reciprocal donation of $200,000 a year for five years. In essence, almost half of Yashin's donation was to be filtered back to his parent's company for the ambiguous "services rendered." The NAC said this side arrangement broke tax laws and refused to agree to it. So Yashin pulled the plug on the deal.

On the ice, Yashin continued to score. He finished the season with a team record of 94 points and finished as runner-up for the Hart Trophy for most valuable player in the NHL.

Despite their success, Yashin and the Senators once again stumbled in the post-season. During the first round of the 1999 playoffs, the tough, hard-checking Buffalo Sabres smothered the team. They limited Alfredsson to three points, while completely silencing Yashin. The Sabres swept the Senators with ease in four games.

Ottawa fans were not happy. Yashin often looked lost on the ice against the Sabres, unable to deal with their aggressive style. Rather than fight through the checking, he seemed resigned to losing. It was as though the player — and the man — lacked self-confidence. He didn't believe he could over-

The Tale of Two Captains

come the Sabres bullies, so he stopped trying.

That being said, Yashin was just one player. It was wrong to pin all the club's woes on him. The Senators were not yet a Stanley Cup contender. Their goaltending was suspect, and while their forwards were fast and talented, they were also small.

Following the 1998-99 campaign, the relationship between Yashin and the Senators reached the breaking point. The Senators were told by Yashin's agent that unless Yashin received a new contract, he would not return to the team. This time, Rod Bryden refused to budge. There would be no bonuses. There would be no renegotiated deal. Senators general manager Marshall Johnson (who replaced Gauthier's successor Rick Dudley in June 1999) told the media, "If Alexei does not deliver a full season of play this year, he will be obligated to deliver to our club a full season in the next year in which he decides to play in the NHL." The Senators gave Yashin until November 8 to re-join the team. Managers around the league, not surprisingly, applauded the Senators for their stance.

Yashin was equally stubborn, and given the relatively short length of an athlete's career and Yashin's burgeoning stardom, this was a risky move by Yashin and Gandler.

Yashin failed to re-join the team on November 8 and was suspended for the entire 1999-2000 season. The suspension did nothing to quiet the soap opera. Everyone had tired of Yashin's antics. He was so loathed that a fan actually filed a lawsuit against the player for holding out on his contract simply for "personal gain and self-enrichment" (it was later dismissed). The NHL, on behalf of the Senators, also filed a grievance against Yashin stating he owed them $7 million in damages.

During Yashin's exile, the Alfredsson era officially began. He was named the new team captain.

In May 2000, Yashin received a major blow in his fight to become a restricted free agent when an independent arbitrator ruled he would still owe the Senators for the missed 1999-2000 season. The Senators now held all the cards. Yashin was not only going nowhere, but he would owe the Senators for every season he missed.

On September 9, a very reluctant Yashin announced he would return to the team for the 2000-01 season. It would be awkward, to say the least. Some of his teammates were still upset over his exodus and wanted answers. Outspoken winger Vaclav Prospal vowed to give Yashin his two cents, and Daniel Alfredsson admitted that Yashin would have to clear the air with his teammates. "If he was committed to play 100 per cent and follow our system, we would want him here," said Alfredsson. "Of course, there would be [some awkwardness], but there's nothing you can't talk about. You have to play with open cards. In the long run, everyone wants to win."

Given Alfredsson's mature and positive handling of the situation, it was no surprise when Jacques Martin announced

The Tale of Two Captains

that Alfredsson would remain team captain. "Daniel has always been a Senator; he has always been a classy person; and he has always been a leader by his play on the ice." Yashin wasn't even named an assistant captain.

To rub salt into Yashin's wound, Rod Bryden continued to pursue Yashin in court for US$930,000 in damages for the lost season.

On the ice, Yashin was booed in almost every city. In fact, during a November 18 home game against the Florida Panthers, some Ottawa fans cheered when Florida's Todd Simpson (a future member of the Senators) pummelled an unsuspecting Yashin with 4:40 left in the game. In the locker room, Simpson commented, "The Senators ownership sent him a message by sitting him out. The courts sent him a message by making him come back to play, and I just think it's time the players sent him a message. A lot of the guys don't agree with what he did, and I was hoping to get a standing ovation from the fans. The fans deserve to see him get his butt kicked around a little bit. I thought they'd enjoy that."

Over time, things quietened down. The booing stopped. Bryden dropped his lawsuit, and Yashin quietly put together another excellent year, leading the Senators to their finest season ever with 40 goals and 88 points. But everyone knew Yashin was scoring those goals for himself, not for the team.

Yashin's lack of enthusiasm was evident come playoff time when he once again pulled his invisible man routine. Despite playing in one of the most heated rivalries in recent

Ottawa Senators

NHL history, Yashin played uninspired hockey and was held to one assist as the Toronto Maple Leafs swept their Ontario rivals in the first round.

Yashin then drew anger from Daniel Alfredsson when he showed up an hour late for the team's final meeting of the season. "I guess it shows how much he cares about this team," Alfredsson told *The Ottawa Sun*. Yashin claimed he didn't know when the meeting was set to take place. It didn't matter. It would be the last Senators meeting Alexei Yashin would be asked to attend.

Two months later, the Yashin era finally came to an end. On June 23, 2001, he was traded to the New York Islanders for gigantic defenceman Zdeno Chara, forward Bill Muckler, and a first round draft pick that turned out to be Ottawa's new hope for the future, Jason Spezza. It was a good deal for everyone involved. The Isles got a much-needed marquee player in Yashin, who in turn, received a lucrative 10-year, US$100-million deal.

The Senators were now Daniel Alfredsson's team. He didn't fail them. On the ice, Alfredsson continued to rack up the points with 71 points in 2002, 79 in 2003, and a career best 80 in 2004.

Off the ice, Alfredsson often went beyond the call of duty. In March 2003, a story leaked out that he had agreed to take a $200,000 reduction in salary so the Senators could meet payroll demands during their troubled season. The modest Alfredsson eventually confirmed the story. "I wanted

The Tale of Two Captains

to keep it behind closed doors; it's not something I want to talk about. The only thing I can say is that I want to help the team win."

The bitter taste towards Yashin lingered until the April 2003 playoffs when the Senators met the New York Islanders in the first round. Yashin played perhaps his finest post-season appearance in leading the Isles to a 3-0 opening game victory over the Senators. But it came with a price. The Senators lost the game because they were too focussed on bashing Yashin. Just seconds into the game, Zdeno Chara knocked Yashin's helmet off. He later smashed the Islander player to the ice twice before the first period was over. At least four other Senators, notably Chris Neil, who hammered Yashin into the boards near the end of the game, put him on his back.

After the first contest, Yashin reverted to his "invisible man" routine and the Senators won the next four games, eliminating the Islanders and finally vanquishing the bitter memories of their former player. Fittingly, Daniel Alfredsson set up the series-clinching goal.

In March 2004, the Senators signed Alfredsson, who was becoming an unrestricted free agent, to a new five-year deal. Daniel Alfredsson, it seemed, would be a Senator for life.

Chapter 6
On the Brink...

After being eliminated by the Toronto Maple Leafs for the third consecutive year, the mood in Ottawa was grim during the summer of 2002. Both the fans and the media demanded change. The common consensus was that the team was not tough enough, they lacked the heart, grit, and drive that players like Toronto's Gary Roberts brought to the ice every shift. Others blamed coach Jacques Martin for his cautious defensive system. It was stifling Ottawa's skilled players. He held too tight a leash on them. Perhaps it was time to admit that Jacques Martin was not the man to lead this team to the Stanley Cup. These were the complaints dominating the Ottawa chat shows and sports columns all through the late spring and summer.

On the Brink...

In June 2003, the Senators hired John Muckler as their new general manager (replacing the retiring Marshall Johnston). Muckler was an experienced hockey man who, along with Glen Sather, helped guide the Edmonton Oilers to five Stanley Cups. Muckler agreed the Senators needed more grit, but he refused to blame Jacques Martin. "Jacques is outstanding," Muckler confirmed.

Before Muckler could worry about new faces, he had to take care of the old ones. Daniel Alfredsson, Chris Phillips, Chris Neil, Sami Salo, Radek Bonk, Karel Rachunek, and Mike Fisher were all in need of new contracts. Meanwhile, Muckler traded Senators' veteran Shawn McEachern to Atlanta and sent Sami Salo to Vancouver for forward Peter Schaefer. By training camp, only Rachunek (whose agent was the infamous Mark Gandler) remained unsigned.

Meanwhile, Senators' owner Rod Bryden — who had been routinely threatening to move the team if he didn't get more support from the city — announced plans to re-finance the team. The Senators were saddled with a $375-million debt that was crippling their ability to compete. This was Bryden's second attempt to find financing. Earlier in the year, Bryden announced he had a limited partnership, but the deal collapsed when one of the partners filed for bankruptcy protection. This time, Bryden said he was starting Senators Sports and Entertainment. The new company, backed by one U.S. investor, would buy out the Senators and Corel Centre and become majority owner. He insisted it was the only way to keep the team from being swallowed by its crippling debt.

Bryden's timing was questionable. The Senators were already heading into the season with a lot of question marks. The last thing they needed was to worry about the stability of the franchise.

The Senators stumbled out of the gate to start the 2002-03 season, but the NHL, not Bryden, was to blame. Due to scheduling conflicts, the team was saddled with an unusual eight-day layoff after only their third game of the season. The players were affected by it. They couldn't find their groove. Heading into a November 9 game against the Boston Bruins, the Senators were an uninspiring 5-5-1. Fans and media started to panic. The familiar "maybe it's time to make a deal" cry flooded the airwaves and papers. It wasn't that the Senators were playing terrible hockey. They just seemed unable to put together quality back-to-back performances.

The game against the Bruins was the lowest point of the season. The 7-1 loss wasn't what bothered fans but rather the uninspired play. The Senators played selfish, apathetic hockey. It was one of their worst performances in recent memory.

The club had more problems off the ice. In early November, it was discovered the team had borrowed $14 million from the NHL to pay its bills. Every reporter wanted to know if the off-ice problems were affecting the team's on-ice performance.

The Senators were determined not to let the loss get the better of them. After the blowout, the team went on a

On the Brink...

10-game unbeaten streak and by the end of December, they were at the top of the Eastern Conference, battling with Dallas for the lead in the overall league standings.

On December 31, Bryden's refinancing plan collapsed. The Senators had no operating capital. The following day, players were told the team couldn't meet its payroll. According to the NHL's collective bargaining agreement, the Senators had two weeks to meet payroll. If they failed, every player would become an unrestricted free agent.

If there were any doubts about the Senators' ability to perform with these off-ice distractions, Marian Hossa put them to rest the following night by scoring a natural hat trick to lead the Senators to an 8-1 thrashing of Atlanta. The Senators record stood at 23-9-5, tops in the NHL.

Off the ice, the news got worse. On January 9, when the Senators filed for bankruptcy protection, the team were put up for sale. The Senators owed $14 million to the NHL, $40 million to the Canadian Imperial Bank of Commerce (CIBC), $50.7 million to Covanta Energy Corporation, and $20 million to FleetBoston Financial. Once the Corel Centre's unpaid bills were added, the Senators faced more than $500 million in debts. Meanwhile, the CIBC and FleetBoston Financial provided the team with $8.8 million to pay the players and keep the Senators afloat.

How did the club accumulate this much debt? The trail led back to the days of Bruce Firestone. Lacking the necessary capital, the team had been skating on credit throughout its existence. Bryden was well known as a risk taker and he had counted on some form of government support to help him out. When the government refused, Bryden found himself in trouble. High taxes, the decreasing value of the Canadian dollar (NHL players are paid in U.S. currency), and the debt itself simply became too much to handle. The Senators had been playing a smoke and mirrors routine with its investors, clients, and the league since its inception, but now the show was over.

Meanwhile, the team continued to play strong hockey. They tumbled a bit in January, but it had more to do with a busy schedule than bankruptcy news. The on-ice rise coincided with the arrival of Marian Hossa. The talented Slovak winger was the Senators' first round draft pick in 1997. Since 1998-99, Hossa's statistics had continually improved, but this year, he took his game to a higher level. He was always a fast skater with incredible puck handling skills; now he added strength to his game. His energetic rushes down the right side were almost impossible to stop. Like a young Gordie Howe, Hossa could hold off a checker with one hand, while stickhandling with the other. By mid-season, Hossa had netted 30 goals and was among the NHL's scoring leaders.

Off the ice, there was finally some good news. On January 14, Rod Bryden announced he and one unnamed investor — believed to be Arby's food chain owner Nelson Peltz — had submitted a bid to buy back the Senators. Bryden's deal, which needed the approval of creditors, was

On the Brink...

Marian Hossa battles for the puck

rumoured to be in the range of $140 million. If the deal was accepted, most of the $166 million owed by the Senators would be written off. If the creditors refused the deal, a new buyer would have to be found.

That night, perhaps inspired by Bryden's news, the Senators continued to roll. Led by Martin Havlat's four points and Patrick Lalime's third straight shutout, the Senators pounded the Tampa Bay Lightning 7-0 before a sold-out Corel Centre crowd.

Ottawa Senators

At the end of January, with the Senators riding near the top of the NHL standings, a new face emerged in the ongoing ownership circus. Toronto-born millionaire Eugene Melnyk announced he was interested in buying the Senators and keeping them in Ottawa. And Melnyk had money. According to Forbes magazine, the president and C.E.O. of the Mississauga-based pharmaceutical company Biovail was the 234th richest person in the world with $1.8 billion. Melnyk was also a big hockey fan and already owned the St. Mike's Majors of the Ontario Hockey League.

While the Senators strolled through February finishing the month with an 8-3-1 record, the ownership issue became somewhat murkier. On February 11, it was announced that Bryden's bid was accepted. It was conditional on the acceptance of a separate deal to buy the Corel Centre and still had be approved in court. But just two weeks later, after defaults and missed deadlines, Bryden's deal fell apart. His U.S. backer had pulled the plug on the bid. This was the end of the road for Rod Bryden.

Fortunately for Ottawa, Eugene Melnyk was waiting in the wings.

While Melnyk — along with six other reported bidders — looked over the Senators' books, the team continued to excel. However, one criticism continued to dog the team: lack of character. The playoffs were the time to bring your best effort and the Senators seemed to lack the necessary killer instinct. In mid-March, John Muckler attempted to answer

On the Brink...

the critics by acquiring tough guys Vaclav Varada and Rob Ray in two separate deals with the Buffalo Sabres. Varada was a notorious pest, a player who loved to aggravate his opponents and draw them into making penalties. Ray, on the other hand, was one of the NHL's great fighters. Just before the March trade deadline passed, Muckler also acquired veteran forward Bryan Smolinski from the Los Angeles Kings. Smolinski was a gifted forward who could be counted on to score 20 goals and provide additional leadership.

Inspired by the new additions, the Senators won 7 out of their final 10 games. Their 3-1 victory over the Toronto Maple Leafs in the final game of the season earned the Senators their first President's Trophy, given to the team with the most points.

The Senators set a team record for wins (52) and points (113) during the 2002-2003 season, and Marian Hossa set a new team record with 45 goals (eclipsing Alexei Yashin's old mark of 44 goals). Heading into the 2003 playoffs, an air of cautious optimism surrounded the team. Everyone knew the Senators were good, but did they have the character to finally take them deeper into the playoffs? If the players had any hope of succeeding, they would not only have to play their best hockey, but do so on a consistent basis. Ottawa fans were hopeful.

The Senators handled both the New York Islanders and Philadelphia Flyers with relative ease and, for the first time in their modern history, they advanced to the Conference finals.

Ottawa Senators

The Senators were now only eight victories away from winning the Stanley Cup.

First, they'd have to get by the New Jersey Devils. This would be no easy task. The Devils, led by one of the top goaltenders in the world, Martin Brodeur, had been to the Stanley Cup finals three times in the past nine years, winning two of them.

It was somewhat fitting that the Senators faced the Devils. Senators coach Jacques Martin had long admired their style and consciously modelled the Senators on the Devils. "When I first came here, I used to watch a lot of Devils games because I wanted to be like them," Martin declared. "They were good defensively, strong as a team, and they were committed. And once they got the puck, they played a puck-possession game."

Meanwhile, the city of Ottawa — which hadn't seen a Stanley Cup in 76 years — was buzzing with anticipation. Throughout the city, buildings, cars, and people were adorned with Senators signs, flags, and jerseys. Even non-hockey fans were caught up in the excitement. A sense of confidence, hope, and community enveloped Ottawa. The city had never felt so alive.

Just prior to game one the Ottawa Senators received a boost when the Ontario Supreme Court conditionally approved Eugene Melnyk's $100-million bid to buy the team. Final approval was contingent on the acceptance of a separate deal to buy the Corel Centre from a New Jersey company

On the Brink...

called Covanta Energy Corp. A Manhattan bankruptcy court would decide the outcome of that deal later in the month.

A year of uncertainties and turmoil had suddenly turned into a dream season. The Senators were on the brink of victory, and win or lose, it appeared the team would remain in Ottawa on a more solid footing.

Heading into game one, many commentators felt that the series would be characterized by tight-checking with few scoring chances, in short: dull. It turned out to be anything but dull. By the 7:23 mark of the first period, Ottawa had already taken a 2-0 lead with goals by Chris Neil and Todd White. The Devils seemed in disarray after White's goal. Ottawa continued to press, but Martin Brodeur made a number of outstanding saves to keep the Devils in the game.

Brodeur's play inspired the Devils. They regrouped in the second period, scoring two late goals to tie the game at 2-2.

The teams exchanged numerous scoring chances in the third, but neither could score. Brodeur, in particular, had to be sharp on an Alfredsson blast from the slot early in the third. A few minutes later he also stopped Martin Havlat on a breakaway.

Thanks to an unlikely source, overtime did not last long. At 3:08 of the extra session, fourth line checker Shaun Van Allen tapped the puck into the Devils net after a nifty give-and-go with Martin Havlat. The Corel Centre erupted.

Incredibly, it was the 12-year veteran's first NHL post-season goal. "As a kid growing up playing road hockey in

Ottawa Senators

Saskatchewan, you dream of scoring an overtime goal," said a jubilant Van Allen after the game. "You just hope it can happen one day."

It was too early to start uncorking the champagne, but the Ottawa Senators were only three victories away from the Stanley Cup finals. If there was a year to make the finals, this was it. Two teams not expected to be in the playoffs, the Mighty Ducks of Anaheim (led by the stellar play of goaltender, J.S. Giguere) and Minnesota Wild, had not only qualified for the post-season, but stunned hockey observers by eliminating Western Conference powerhouses Colorado, Detroit, and Vancouver. The Ducks and Wild were now facing each other in the Western Conference finals. Despite their Cinderella success, most spectators felt the winner of the Eastern final would be a sure bet to win the Cup.

Then the unthinkable happened: the Senators collapsed. The Devils not only registered a decisive 4-1 victory in game two; they also took games three (1-0) and four (5-2). Just like that, the Devils were up three games to one. The Senators suddenly found themselves on the brink of elimination.

The city fell silent. With their scorers (Hossa, Alfredsson, and Havlat) not scoring, there seemed little chance the Senators could mount a comeback and win three consecutive games against the mighty Devils. The familiar "one game at a time" motto was heard throughout the city, but few really believed the Senators could do it.

On the Brink...

Senators assistant coach Roger Neilson, who was fighting two types of cancer and would not live through the summer, sat in a chair in the middle of the dressing room prior to game five. In a quiet, trembling voice, the frail coach spoke to the players about seizing the opportunities that life had placed in front of them. The room was deathly quiet as Neilson's powerful words resonated with each player. "This might be your chance, so take it."

The Senators did just that. Inspired by Neilson's speech, along with the presence of rookie Jason Spezza, who was cheered every time he touched the puck, the Senators displayed much more intensity and focus in game five.

After a scoreless opening period, the teams exchanged goals in the second. With the score tied 1-1, Martin Havlat jammed the puck under goaltender Martin Brodeur and into the crease. As Brodeur tried to trap the puck with his glove, it slid into the net. Jason Spezza drew an assist on the play, much to the delight of Ottawa fans.

Five minutes later, Spezza sent the Corel Centre crowd into a frenzy when he tipped a Chris Phillips shot behind Brodeur. The Senators held on for a 3-1 victory.

It was a storybook night for Spezza, who assisted on the winning goal and added the insurance marker. Spezza's heroics made headlines throughout the country. Even his teammates were impressed. "He came in and played awesome," Daniel Alfredsson stated. "It is a very tough situation...and he handled it real well, I thought. He worked

Jason Spezza

himself great into the game, made smart plays and played with poise."

Thanks to Neilson and Spezza, the Senators had life.

"One game at a time; one game at a time," the city whispered.

Game six moved back to New Jersey. The veteran Devils

On the Brink...

were upset with their play in game five and vowed to do better. "You could tell they wanted it more than we did," pronounced Devils' forward Joe Nieuwendyck after game five. "That's unacceptable, but we're gonna get it in gear tomorrow and make sure we play game six like it's a game seven."

Both teams were ready for game six. The Senators had a slight edge in play during a fast-paced but scoreless first period. Their best chance came midway through the first when Brodeur deflected an attempted pass by Radek Bonk to a wide-open Vaclav Varada.

Radek Bonk gave the Senators a 1-0 lead on a power play goal late in the second period. The Devils drew even early in the third with a power play goal of their own by Joe Nieuwendyck — who had missed on at least three other excellent chances earlier in the game.

The Devils ran into penalty trouble midway through the third period after penalties to Jamie Langenbrunner and defenceman Brian Rafalski gave Ottawa a 17-second two-man advantage. During the power play, the Senators put one shot off the right post and another off the crossbar.

A few minutes after the penalties, Brodeur got lucky again as he just managed to tip a Magnus Arvedson backhander off the right post and out.

While both goalies performed exceptionally in overtime, Lady Luck was also on their side. A few minutes after Lalime made a nice glove save on a Brian Gionta wrist shot, Jeff Friesen came within inches of eliminating the Senators, but his deflection went just wide of the right post. Later in overtime, Daniel Alfredsson dashed down the left side and backhanded a shot over Brodeur's right shoulder and off the left post.

With just over five minutes remaining in the first overtime period, Marian Hossa got around defenceman Scott Stevens and threw the puck at the net. Parked alone in front, Vaclav Varada was stopped twice by Brodeur before Chris Phillips squeezed in and finally pushed the puck into the Devils net.

Phillips' goal brought Ottawa fans — and most Canadians — out of their seats. It was the high point of Phillips' career, a shot that gave the Senators a second chance and allowed the city of Ottawa a chance to dream of winning the Stanley Cup. No longer could cynics question the character of the Ottawa Senators.

After climbing two intimidating mountains, the Senators headed home for game seven with momentum on their side. Could they answer the bell one more time?

Before the Senators came onto the ice for game seven, the roar of the 18,500 towel-waving fans was deafening. The building literally shook. They had the home advantage. This is what the Senators had fought for all season long, and now they were seeing the fruits of that 82-game labour.

The crowd was barely able to find their seats before Magnus Arvedson gave the Senators a 1-0 lead on a shot that beat Brodeur stick side just three minutes into the game. A

On the Brink...

sea of white flooded the arena as fans spun their towels into a tornado of frenzied approval. Feeding off the electricity of the crowd, the Senators dominated the first 10 minutes of the opening period.

The Devils regained their composure midway through the period and began to take the play to the Senators. Patrick Lalime was on top of his game when he stopped John Madden on a partial breakaway late in the first.

The Devils carried their momentum into the second period. Then, in under two minutes, Jamie Langenbrunner sent the Corel Centre crowd into a stunned silence when he scored two goals to give the Devils a 2-1 lead.

Jacques Martin immediately called a timeout to settle the team down. This also gave the fans a chance to overcome their shock, and they began waving their white flags frantically in support of the Senators.

The break seemed to work. The team returned to the ice more focussed. For the remainder of the period, the Senators' tempo increased as their forecheckers continued to force the slower Devils defence. With 30 seconds to go in the second period, Ottawa's speed forced the Devils' Colin White to take a slashing penalty.

The Senators failed to capitalize on the power play but Alfredsson, Hossa, and Rachunek all had good chances to score. As the Devils' Jeff Friesen entered the Ottawa zone, Karel Rachunek poke checked the puck from him towards centre ice. Marian Hossa picked it up at centre and broke in over the Devils' blue line. He sent a pass over Radek Bonk, who wired a one-timer past Brodeur. The Corel Centre exploded. A disgusted Friesen smashed his stick in anger. The game was tied 2-2.

For the remainder of the period, the Senators continued to press the Devils. It seemed like only a matter of time before Ottawa took the lead. At the very least, it appeared the teams were once again heading for overtime.

Then, with just over two minutes to play, Jeff Friesen dumped the puck towards the left side of centre ice. Winger Grant Marshall collected it at centre and skated towards the Senators zone. As Marshall raced down the left side, both Ottawa defencemen (Rachunek and Wade Redden) converged on him. What they didn't realize was that Friesen was wide open and headed towards the Senators goal. Marshall quickly fired the puck over to Friesen. Redden, realizing his mistake, raced back to check Friesen before the puck reached him. But as he turned, he stumbled slightly. Friesen collected the pass. He then deked to the left on Senators goalie Patrick Lalime, and shot the puck just over Lalime's pads and into the Ottawa net.

The Corel Centre fell deadly silent.

It should never have happened. It was a routine play gone askew.

Friesen had his redemption; the Devils had earned a visit to the Stanley Cup finals.

The Ottawa players were stunned. When time expired,

On the Brink...

Rachunek and Hossa collapsed to the ice. Phillips held his head in his hands.

To come so close to the dream, only to see it snatched from their sticks, was a nightmare. As much as the Senators wanted to win for themselves and the city, they also wanted this for Roger Neilson. With his health rapidly failing, the team knew this might be his last chance at a Stanley Cup. As it turned out, Neilson passed away a month later.

Before the team left the ice, the appreciative fans rose one last time to give their heroes a standing ovation.

Somewhere down the road, the players would find solace in the knowledge that they overcame numerous on- and off-ice obstacles to make it to within one game, one goal of the Stanley Cup finals.

They had silenced those who had questioned the heart and character of the Ottawa Senators.

Chapter 7
Battle of Ontario

From a Toronto perspective, it wasn't much of a battle. The Maple Leafs had beaten the Senators in the playoffs every year they had met. If anything, the Battle of Ontario had become a condition, a psychosis. The Maple Leafs were the id to the Senators' ego, the monsters lurking in the shadows of their rooms.

No team has had more influence on the psyche of the Ottawa Senators than the Toronto Maple Leafs. Even though the Senators were playing top-notch hockey during the regular season, one loss to the Maple Leafs triggered anxiety and panic throughout the city and led to questions over the character and toughness of the team.

Battle of Ontario

The most common complaint following a loss to the Leafs was that the Senators lacked the hard-working ethic of the Leafs. The Senators management seemed to agree. Following regular season losses to the Leafs in 2003 and 2004, general manager John Muckler added tough, gritty players to the roster. He denied these moves were made in response to a single team, but clearly there was concern in the Senators' front office that their skilled team needed more of an edge.

It took eight seasons for the Battle of Ontario to begin, but when it did, it instantly became one of hockey's fiercest rivalries. The rivalry was so intense that, at times, it seemed that beating the Toronto Maple Leafs in the playoffs was more important to Ottawa fans than winning the Stanley Cup.

During the Senators' first six years in the NHL, there wasn't much of a rivalry between Toronto and Ottawa. The teams only met twice each season and the Senators were simply not competitive enough to generate a rivalry. Ottawa was also home to a huge Leafs fan base. (To this day, Maple Leafs' goals are greeted with a disturbingly loud roar in Ottawa). Ottawa just didn't care enough about their own team just yet.

Attitudes began to change when the Leafs moved to the Senators' division during the 1998-99 season. Leafs president Ken Dryden had pressured the league for years to put Toronto in the same division as Ottawa and Montreal. The NHL finally agreed in 1998. The Senators and Leafs would now meet four times a year.

Ottawa Senators

Initially, the rivalry was one-sided. Hugh Adami of *The Ottawa Citizen* likened the fledgling Ottawa team to the attention-seeking Chester in the old Warner Brothers cartoon, while Toronto was the uninterested bulldog, Spike. ("Hey Spike! Hey Spike! Whatcha wanna do today?")

In 2000, Toronto began to take notice of Ottawa. A request from Bryden for government aid was unpopular with the Maple Leafs organization and the Toronto media who felt the initiative was just an excuse for the financially struggling Senators to get a free handout. Toronto's anger towards Ottawa was further fuelled during a March 11 game when a carefree swing at the puck by Ottawa's Marian Hossa caught Toronto's Bryan Berard in the right eye. Berard fell to the ice, his eye bleeding profusely. It was later discovered that Berard had lost some of his sight. His career was in jeopardy (after a year off, Berard returned to the NHL). While it was clearly an accident, the incident triggered the beginning of Toronto coach Pat Quinn's jabs at the Senators for being a scared and dirty team.

One month later, the Senators and Maple Leafs found themselves facing off in their first-ever playoff series. The Battle of Ontario was born.

Battle of Ontario I
The Leafs finished the 1999-2000 season just five points ahead of the Senators with 100 points. The teams met five times during the season, with Ottawa outplaying the Leafs

Battle of Ontario

and coming away with a 3-1-1 record.

The two teams couldn't have been more different. The Leafs, led by Mats Sundin, Steve Thomas, Darcy Tucker, Tie Domi, Igor Korolev, and Sergei Berezin were a mix of skill and grit. Thomas Kaberle and Dmitry Yushkevich led an inconsistent Leafs blue line that was weakened late in the season by the loss of budding star Bryan Berard. The cornerstone for the Leafs was their goalie, Curtis Joseph. He turned away almost 2000 shots during the season and had a stellar .915 save percentage.

The Senators were a young, fast, and skilled team led by Radek Bonk, Daniel Alfredsson, Marian Hossa, and Magnus Arvedson. Their speedy forwards relied on an aggressive forecheck to cause turnovers and create scoring chances. Wade Redden, Igor Kravchuk, Jason York, Sami Salo, and Chris Phillips provided the Senators with a solid defensive core capable of moving the puck quickly out of their zone. The weakness of the defence was their lack of toughness and size in front of their own net.

In goal, the fate of the Senators rested on veteran Tom Barrasso, who was acquired from the Pittsburgh Penguins in March. The club hoped the two-time Stanley Cup-winning Barrasso would be the goalie to take them deep into the playoffs. It was Barrasso versus Joseph. The Senators knew if they had any hope of winning the series, they needed to beat Joseph. "There's no secret about that," said Ottawa's Wade Redden. "We have to find a way to get more by [Joseph] than

Ottawa Senators

Radek Bonk

they get by us, and that's going to be tough because he's such a great goalie." Senators forwards would have to get in close and create turmoil around Joseph's crease.

In game one, things got nasty almost immediately: Ottawa defenceman Grant Ledyard blind-sided Leafs tough guy Tie Domi with an open ice hit; Ottawa's Daniel Alfredsson jabbed the back of Darcy Tucker's knee after Tucker scored the first goal; Garry Valk later speared Alfredsson; the Leafs' Yanic Perreault suffered a knee injury after being

Battle of Ontario

kneed by an Ottawa player.

If it wasn't hate, it was pretty darn close.

Surprisingly, it was the Senators who played undisciplined hockey. Magnus Arvedson went off for hooking only 1:26 into the game. About four minutes later, Radek Bonk took two unnecessary penalties. The Senators didn't get their first shot on goal until just past the midway point of the first period. Fortunately, they managed to get out of the first period unscathed.

In the second, the Senators came on stronger, outshooting the Leafs 10-2 in the first eight minutes. Curtis Joseph, in the Leafs goal, was sensational, stopping Joe Juneau and Magnus Arvedson, and later Chris Phillips and Vaclav Prospal. Joseph's brilliance seemed to take the wind out of the Senators' attack. A minor penalty put an end to the onslaught. Toronto took full advantage of the power play as Darcy Tucker scored to give the Leafs a 1-0 lead.

The Senators stayed out of the box in the third period, but with the exception of a Radek Bonk shot off the post with five minutes to go, they couldn't beat Joseph. With 21 seconds left, Mats Sundin, who hadn't scored a goal in two years against the Senators, iced the victory with an empty net goal.

Game two was close for about 20 minutes. The Leafs came out hitting in the second period and exploded for three goals in the first 3:30. Their physical play put the Senators on their heels and the Leafs cruised to a 5-1 win.

Off the ice, the media wondered if the trade for Barrasso

had been a mistake. While Barrasso was being peppered by the Maple Leafs, former Senators' goalie Ron Tugnutt was leading the Pittsburgh Penguins to a 2-0 series lead over Washington. The criticism was a little unfair. Certainly he looked slow on a couple of goals, but should Barrasso also be blamed for the Senators' lack of offence? After two games, they'd beaten Joseph only once.

Barrasso silenced the critics in game three. His 33-save performance helped the Senators get back in the series with a 4-3 win over the Leafs. Although the Senators only had three shots in the first period, they scored once. When the Leafs did get their chances, Barrasso was there. He robbed Sergei Berezin and Mats Sundin, the latter with a spectacular diving save using his goal stick.

Play evened out in the second. Rob Zamuner put the Senators up 2-0 on only their fifth shot of the game, only to have Toronto's Steve Thomas respond just 19 seconds later.

Colin Forbes gave Ottawa a 3-1 lead five minutes into the third period and then Dmitri Khristich responded at 10:18 to bring the Leafs to within a goal. The Leafs continued to put pressure on the Senators, but Barrasso was at his best. With five minutes to play, Rob Zamuner scored on a soft shot through traffic. Joseph tried to make the save, but his left pad was blocked by the skate of Senators captain Daniel Alfredsson, who was battling Toronto defenceman Cory Cross at the side of the net. After the puck crossed the line, an incensed Joseph threw his blocker to the ice and chased ref-

Battle of Ontario

eree Mick McGeough into the corner. While in pursuit, Joseph stumbled and slid into McGeough, causing both men to fall to the ice. Joseph was given a 10-minute misconduct for the play and faced a possible suspension. Joseph felt that Alfredsson had interfered with him. McGeough argued that it was Cross who had forced Alfredsson into the net. Toronto's Jonas Hoglund scored with 17 seconds left, but the Senators held on for the win.

In game four, Andreas Dackell, not known for his goal scoring, banked Ottawa's only goals as the Senators evened the series at 2-2. Once again, the Senators were heavily outshot by the Leafs, but Barrasso continued to shine.

With Ottawa back in the series, the pressure intensified between the two teams. Toronto's Tie Domi and Ottawa's Andre Roy were hitting, shoving, and yapping at each other both on the ice and in the media. "The guy's a clown," declared Domi about Roy.

Darcy Tucker then became public enemy #1 in Ottawa when he suggested that if the Senators could interfere with Curtis Joseph, he'd do the same to Tom Barrasso. "If someone pushes me, I'll keep going into Barrasso," Tucker told the Toronto media.

Game five turned out to be the best game of the series. Both teams had excellent chances to score. Four minutes in, a blast by Toronto's Igor Korolev missed the Ottawa net by inches. A few seconds later, Barrasso robbed Korolev with a beautiful sliding pad save. Marian Hossa found himself alone

Ottawa Senators

in front of Joseph, but lost control of the puck. Finally, Senators' forward Joe Juneau — driving to the net — scored to give the Senators a 1-0 lead. Seconds later, Steve Thomas beat Barrasso but hit the post.

Juneau's goal held up for the entire second period as the stingy Senators reverted to their defensive game and successfully shut down the Leafs' forwards.

With 12 minutes to go in the third period, Tie Domi went off for interference. A minute and a half later, Gary Valk was nailed with a double minor for high sticking. It was a golden opportunity for the Senators to put the game away, but they failed. The Leafs seemed to gain momentum from their penalty kill and continued to apply pressure.

With 4:30 remaining in regulation time, Steve Thomas sent a drop pass from Mats Sundin over the left shoulder of Barrasso. It was only the Leafs' second shot of the period. The game was tied 1-1 and headed for overtime.

The Leafs continued to press in the extra period, averaging almost a shot per minute at goal. Barrasso was phenomenal, stopping the Leafs at every turn. Early in overtime, Barrasso once again robbed Korolev. Ten minutes later, he stopped Darcy Tucker from in close. The most spectacular save came moments later when Barrasso slid across the crease and stacked the pads to rob Adam Mair.

The contest finally came to end when Steve Thomas raced to catch up with Sergei Berezin and create a two-on-one opportunity. Berezin, who never met a shot he didn't like,

Battle of Ontario

surprised everyone in the building, including himself, by passing to Thomas, who slid a backhand past a sprawling Tom Barrasso.

The Senators had blown it. For almost three full periods, the Senators had played textbook defensive hockey. They had the Battle of Ontario under lock and key, but their lack of killer instinct had cost them. They had played their best game of the series and it wasn't enough.

With the Leafs only one game away from eliminating the Senators, Ottawa had no choice but to rebound from the heartbreaking defeat.

As promised, the Senators came out flying in game six. Joe Juneau kept the rowdy home crowd energized when he put home a Shawn McEachern rebound at 3:30 to give his team an early lead. Igor Kravchuk put the Senators up 2-0 early in the second period. The club seemed to have the game under control, but then it all fell apart. Twelve seconds after Kravchuk's goal, Ottawa's Sami Salo (who was on the ice for all four of Toronto's goals) gave the puck up to Steve Thomas, who beat Barrasso with a wrist shot.

Just over three minutes later, Thomas fired a shot that bounced off Kravchuk and landed at the feet of Mats Sundin, who fired the shot into an empty Senators net.

Two and half minutes after Sundin's goal, Sergei Berezin capitalized on a weak clearing attempt by Salo and scored on a power play, and the Leafs were ahead 3-2. Before the second period was over, Wendel Clark beat Barrasso to give

Ottawa Senators

Toronto a comfortable two-goal lead.

The Senators pressed in the final period, but Curtis Joseph stood his ground and preserved the series win for the Leafs.

The mood in Ottawa was sour. Senators' coach Jacques Martin blamed inexperience on the loss. The bigger concern was the team's lack of intensity. They had the Leafs down and out in game five and they failed to put the nail in the coffin.

Battle of Ontario II

The two teams squared off again during the first round of the 2001 playoffs. The mood, though, was different. The Senators had dominated the Leafs during the regular season, winning all five games. Led by Alexei Yashin — who returned after a season-long holdout — Ottawa finished 19 points better than the Leafs in the standings. Even the Toronto media believed the Senators were too good for the Leafs this time around. "The way Toronto has been playing the past two months, I can't see them winning," Leafs' broadcaster Harry Neale told *The Ottawa Citizen*.

The key for the Senators would be Yashin and newcomer Patrick Lalime. Lalime's first season as the Senators' goalie had been a resounding success, but he had no playoff experience. Would he be able to handle the pressure? Yashin, meanwhile, had put together yet another solid regular season but could he finally overcome his annual invisible man act in the playoffs?

Battle of Ontario

The answers came fast.

The Senators played strong during the first period of game one and outshot the Leafs 12-3, but they couldn't beat Curtis Joseph. It was the Leafs, however, who hit hardest in the first period. Toronto's Tie Domi blindsided rookie Martin Havlat with a vicious check at centre ice. Havlat was down on the ice for several minutes before being escorted to the dressing room.

In the second period, the Senators continued to dominate, but again, couldn't score. The Leafs fared no better. The closest they came to the Ottawa net was when Bryan McCabe flattened Lalime.

Play heated up a little in the third. Joseph stopped Hossa once with eight minutes remaining and then again in the final minute. Lalime made a nice pad save off Senators' killer Steve Thomas with two seconds left in regulation time.

The Senators had a brief scare with five minutes remaining when Nik Antropov scored off a Sergei Berezin rebound. The goal was waved off when it was ruled that Antropov's stick was too high.

Once again, the two teams headed for overtime. At 10:49 of overtime, Mats Sundin unleashed a shot from just outside the left faceoff circle that just hit the inside of the far goalpost. Toronto was up 1-0 in the series.

The Senators fared no better in game two. Just 2:49 into the game, Sergei Berezin gave the Leafs a 1-0 lead and they never looked back. Gary Roberts added goals in the second and third, and for the second straight game, the Senators were shut out. They were an abysmal 0-11 on the power play and Toronto's Shayne Corson had done an effective — albeit easy — job of nullifying Alexei Yashin, who once again showed no determination or passion.

For the first 57 minutes of game three, the Senators were lifeless. Heading into the final five minutes of the game, the Maple Leafs had a comfortable 2-0 lead. But with 3:09 remaining, Marian Hossa took control.

Hossa skated around a fallen Yushkevich, faked out Curtis Joseph, and put the puck in the net. It was his first NHL playoff point. Alexei Yashin got an assist, his first point in seven playoff games. The goal also ended Joseph's shutout string against the Senators at 223 minutes and 41 seconds.

With Lalime off for an extra attacker, Daniel Alfredsson — as usual, the hardest working Senator of the night — took an improbable shot from the left boards that found its way through the maze of traffic and past Joseph. With 36 seconds left, the Senators tied the game.

The teams headed for overtime again, but it didn't last long. At 2:16, Leafs' defenceman Cory Cross pounced on a rebound off a shot from Nik Antropov and put it past Lalime.

The goal was crushing for the Senators. They had blown a golden opportunity once again. They were now down 3-0 in the series. The players talked the talk, but everyone knew that unless the Senators performed a major miracle, it was over.

For a moment in game four, the Senators had hope.

Battle of Ontario

Chris Phillips, returning from an injury, gave his club a 1-0 lead at 2:30 of the opening period. The lead was brief. With Alfredsson in the penalty box, Yanic Perreault scored to tie the game. Ten minutes later, after Ottawa's Rob Zamuner had just missed an empty net, Perreault scored again. The Senators seemed to deflate after that goal. They were unable to mount any sort of sustained attack for the rest of the game. When Bryan McCabe put the Leafs up by two with ten minutes to go in the game, Leafs fans tossed brooms on the ice to signal the sweep.

For three straight years, the Senators were eliminated in the first round. This year was a particularly tough pill to swallow, because Ottawa had finished with their best regular season record ever.

Ottawa fans and media were angry. "There's a fury out there I haven't heard before," said one Ottawa radio host. Many fans said they wouldn't renew their season tickets if Jacques Martin came back as coach. The fans were right to be angry. It wasn't just that the Senators had lost in the first round, again, it was the way they lost that angered people. At various times they looked inept, apathetic, and lost. Alexei Yashin, in particular, looked like he was sleepwalking.

For two straight years, Toronto had put an end to the Senators' Stanley Cup hopes.

They had become Ottawa's nightmare.

Ottawa Senators

Battle of Ontario III

The Senators and Maple Leafs met up for the third straight year in 2001-02, this time during the Conference semi-finals. Going into the series, the Maple Leafs had played an extremely tough seven-game series against the New York Islanders, while the Senators made it past the first round with a convincing five-game victory over the Philadelphia Flyers.

The Senators were favoured to beat the Maple Leafs. The Senators had shaken the first round "monkey" off their backs against the Flyers. Patrick Lalime shutout the Flyers in three straight games, and for once, their star players (Hossa, Bonk, and Havlat) all showed up and shook off their reputations as playoff busts.

The Leafs, meanwhile, were tired and hurting. Mats Sundin and Dmitry Yushkevich were out with injuries and Curtis Joseph was still recovering from a broken hand.

But if Senators fans expected a tea party, they were in for a surprise. "People say there was a lot of hate in the Islanders series," claimed Maple Leafs' Tie Domi. "Well, there's going to be a lot of hate in the Ottawa series."

Domi was right, but little did he know it would start off the ice. A month earlier, controversial TV commentator Don Cherry angered the mayor of Ottawa when he announced on national television that Ottawa manager Marshall Johnson "wouldn't know a hockey player if he tripped over Bobby Orr."

Mayor Bob Chiarelli's angry response was, "I know he's

Battle of Ontario

great for ratings in the Toronto area, but he's quite insulting and unacceptable for the sports fans here in Ottawa." Chiarelli went on to suggest that Hockey Night in Canada's on-air personalities were being "coached" to favour Toronto in order to keep the ratings up in the country's largest market. Hockey Night in Canada's producer Ron Darling told Chiarelli to stick to politics.

The previous year, Chiarelli (echoing the feelings of many people outside of Toronto) had accused Hockey Night in Canada's broadcasting team of Bob Cole and Harry Neale of having a pro-Toronto bias. Neale, who denied any favouritism, had this to say at the time, "If it isn't good enough for Ottawa, they can take a big bite of my ass."

The Leafs came out hard early in game one, but their undisciplined play cost them dearly. Alexander Mogilny took a four-minute high sticking penalty at 7:15 of the first period and the Senators' power play unit scored twice. First, Martin Havlat silenced the Maple Leaf crowd when he scored to give the Senators a 1-0 lead. Just over a minute later, Radek Bonk, on a nice feed from Havlat, put the Senators up by two. Before the period ended, defenceman Shane Hnidy made it 3-0. The slaughter was on.

Just 1:40 into the second period, Todd White gave Ottawa a 4-0 lead. Daniel Alfredsson made it 5-0 midway through the period when he scored while the Leafs were two men down. That was more than enough for the Senators to take a 1-0 lead in the series.

Ottawa Senators

Game two was a much closer affair. The Senators started out well, but by the six-minute mark of the first, the Leafs capitalized on two Senators miscues and jumped to a 2-0 lead.

But the Senators remained calm and eventually crawled their way back into the game. Sami Salo made it 2-1 at 7:52 of the second period. Then, just under three minutes into the third period, Mike Fisher tied it with a goal reminiscent of Alfredsson's game-tying playoff goal against the Leafs in 2001. From the left boards, Fisher released a wrist shot, just hoping to get the puck on net. To everyone's surprise, the puck sailed over Joseph's shoulder and into the short side of the net.

For the third time in their playoff history, the two teams were heading to overtime.

The Leafs out-chanced the Senators in the first overtime, but failed to beat Lalime.

Play picked up considerably in the second overtime. Brunet, Salo, and Shawn McEachern all forced Joseph to make good saves, while Lalime robbed Robert Reichel from in close before thanking his lucky stars when a Darcy Tucker shot ringed off the goal post.

The longest game in Senators history finally came to an end at 4:30 of the third overtime. Gary Roberts won a faceoff in the Senators zone, jumped on the loose puck, and quickly fired it past a surprised Lalime. Just like that, the Leafs were back in the series.

Battle of Ontario

Cheered on by a supportive Ottawa crowd, the Senators bounced back in game three and won 3-2 to take a 2-1 series lead.

The Leafs, who had developed a reputation across the league as a team of whiners, were upset after the game. Joseph was irate over Alfredsson's eventual game winner, claiming that Benoit Brunet had interfered with him. Joseph was careful with his words, but clearly he felt that referee Brad Watson had it in for the Leafs. He was the same referee who awarded the New York Islanders a penalty shot late in game four of the Leafs-Islanders series.

Tie Domi was more blunt. "[Watson] doesn't have to come out and answer questions about his mistake. He doesn't have to come out here and be accountable. [Brunet] hit Joseph with his stick. You've got to avoid contact. That's the call. We've got to come out here and answer to you [reporters]. If we don't come out and talk to you guys, we get fined, but he doesn't have to come out and answer to this bullshit."

Controversial officiating carried over into game four. Despite playing a dreadful first period, the Senators managed to keep the game tied at 1-1 in the second period.

Alyn McCauley scored his second goal of the night to give the Leafs a 2-1 lead at the end of two periods.

The Senators came out hard in the third period, but the Leafs managed to hold them off. Enter controversy. With 25 seconds remaining, the Senators appeared to have scored and referee Kevin Pollack signalled a goal. The Leafs asked Pollack for a video review to determine if the Senators had in fact scored during a huge scrum in front of Joseph. The play was ruled inconclusive. There was no evidence, according to officials, that the puck had crossed the line. Ottawa fans were livid. They booed the decision and littered the ice with debris. The Leafs held onto to a 2-1 victory. Heading back to Toronto, the series was now tied at 2-2.

In game five, Wade Redden gave the Senators an early lead before Gary Roberts deflected a shot by Lalime in the dying seconds of the first period. Marian Hossa — who was finally playing up to his potential — then gave the Senators a 2-1 lead 7:13 into the second period. The score stayed that way until just over the midway point of the third period when Alyn McCauley jammed home a Gary Roberts rebound with 7:26 left in regulation.

With just over two minutes left and the game heading towards overtime, Daniel Alfredsson smashed the Leaf's pesky centre, Darcy Tucker, into the boards. Tucker went in face first and then crumpled to the ice. Alfredsson headed towards the net, took a pass from Juha Ylonen, and fired it past Joseph. Neither referee called a penalty on Alfredsson's hit. Leaf fans — echoing the events of game four — went crazy and littered the ice with garbage.

Radek Bonk followed with an empty net goal and the Senators prevailed with a thrilling 4-2 victory.

After the game, the Alfredsson hit was all the talk. Game

Alfredsson in front, Radek Bonk behind.

officials said that Alfredsson hit Tucker "on the shoulder" from the side, before he spun into the boards. Alfredsson, naturally, agreed.

The Leafs were stunned. "I'm quite frankly full of anger," spat Leafs' head coach Pat Quinn. Leafs' president Ken Dryden called the non-call "totally unjust."

It was a moot point. The clocks could not go back. The cold, hard fact was the Ottawa Senators were one game away from finally exorcising their demons and eliminating the Toronto Maple Leafs.

In game six, the Senators came out determined to put down the Leafs once and for all. Goals by Hossa and

Ottawa Senators

Alfredsson put the Senators up 2-0 just 4:39 into game five. The Leafs didn't get their first shot on net until the midway point of the first period. The Leafs looked shaky and confused. They were scrambling around, playing undisciplined hockey. Panic appeared to have set in.

Then came the turning point in the series. Ottawa's Ricard Persson — who was filling in for the injured Zdeno Chara — was assessed a five-minute penalty and a game misconduct for hitting Tie Domi from behind into the boards. The call was as questionable as the game five non-call against Alfredsson. At best, Persson's hit warranted a two-minute minor. Replays suggest that Domi slightly embellished the impact. Either way, the penalty proved costly.

Bryan McCabe made it 2-1 just 20 seconds into the power play and then Gary Roberts (who had an outstanding series) tied the game just before Persson's major came to an end. After soaring out the gates, the Senators suddenly found themselves saddled with a 2-2 tie and a swing in momentum.

Roberts struck again in the second period, giving the Leafs a 3-2 lead, but with just 25 seconds remaining, Todd White evened the score.

Alexander Mogilny put the Leafs up for good just 4:28 into the third period.

The Senators never recovered from the Persson penalty. In game seven, they played their worst game of the playoffs as Toronto finished off the Senators for the third straight year with a 3-0 victory.

Battle of Ontario

What made the loss all the more painful was that the Senators were playing an injury-depleted Leafs lineup. The Leafs played the entire series without, among others, their star Mats Sundin. Their defensive corps was weakened, and thanks to Alfredsson's game five hit, Darcy Tucker missed the final two games. But players like Bryan McCabe, Alex Mogilny, Gary Roberts, and Alyn McCauley turned up their games a notch, playing with incredible grit and determination. In the end, the Leafs seemed to want it more than the Senators.

Intermission
The teams didn't meet in the playoffs during the 2002-03 season, but that didn't stop the rivalry from gaining more fuel. The season series featured tight checking, intense, and respectful games, but none of them matched the viciousness of their playoff games. That is, until March 4, 2003.

With Ottawa up 3-1 near the midway point of the third period, Ottawa's Chris Neil checked Toronto's Travis Green. Green then boarded Shane Hnidy. While the play continued, Neil started shouting at Tucker from the Ottawa bench. An incensed Tucker skated over to the Ottawa bench. What happened next remains a mystery. Leafs' coach, Pat Quinn claimed, "The kid [Neil] spit on [Tucker]."

"I didn't spit on anyone," Neil replied. "I guess Tucker, Corson, and Green are pretty tight, so if you do something to one they're all on you."

Ottawa Senators

Whatever the cause, Tucker blew a gasket, jumped into the Senators bench and attacked Neil. Several Senators joined in and this caused Quinn to start slamming a stick against the glass partition separating the two teams. A Senators' trainer responded by tossing a towel and water bottle back at the Leafs bench.

Tucker ended up with minors for instigating and roughing, two majors for fighting, a 10-minute misconduct, and two game misconducts. This followed a charging penalty called against Toronto's Travis Green.

Then, with less than two minutes remaining, Tie Domi jumped an unsuspecting Magnus Arvedson. Domi received a roughing minor, instigator, fighting major, misconduct, and game misconduct.

Ottawa won the game 4-1.

The NHL had the final say in the matter, suspending Tucker for five games and Domi for three.

Domi later came out and blasted the Senators in the press. "The Senators have done a lot of grumbling. They're a bunch of prima donnas, but we know where they're coming from, they've been doing that for the past three years in the playoffs. That's how they are. They like to talk a lot. We do our talking on the ice. That team has no respect for anybody, and until they start getting respect from their opponents and peers, they're not going to go anywhere."

Unfortunately, the rematch never took place. While the Senators came within a goal of the Stanley Cup finals, the

Battle of Ontario

Philadelphia Flyers knocked off the Leafs in the first round.

Battle of Ontario IV
The 2003-04 regular season was, again, filled with memorable Battle of Ontario moments. During a January 9, 7-1 rout of Toronto, Daniel Alfredsson angered the Leafs after he broke his stick and then faked throwing it in the stands. Two nights earlier, the NHL had suspended Mats Sundin for throwing his stick into the crowd. Pat Quinn was incensed. "If you're going to try and show somebody up, you better be ready to pay the price down the line."

"It wasn't meant to be anything bad," replied Alfredsson.

Less than a month later, hostilities between the two teams reached new levels. The Leafs, clearly embarrassed by the 7-1 pounding in January, came out hard at the Senators. Owen Nolan drove Jason Spezza into the boards and out of the game; Ed Belfour slashed any Senator near his crease; and Bryan McCabe gave Marian Hossa a nasty elbow to the face. And that was just the appetizer.

With less than a minute remaining and the Leafs leading 5-1, Tie Domi went after Ottawa's Shaun Van Allen and wrestled him to the ice. Toronto's Nathan Perrott then went off for five minutes for charging. Ottawa's Shane Hnidy later tried to hunt down Perrott in the corridor after the game.

Van Allen accused Domi of gouging him. "I don't care if a guy runs at me, just don't gouge me when I'm down on the ice."

Domi denied the accusation and claimed he was giving Van Allen payback for butt-ending Sundin and spearing Leafs' goalie Ed Belfour. "I've got over 3000 penalty minutes. I don't need to gouge people."

In the eyes of the media, the game was a step backwards for the Senators, who were supposed to be a much tougher team. The Leafs had come at them hard and they had failed to respond. As one broadcaster commented, "The Leafs thought they were in a street fight and the Senators thought it was a pillow fight."

Six days later, the two teams met again in what turned out to be one of the strangest hockey games of recent memory. The Senators built up a 4-0 lead in the first period only to see it evaporate into a 5-4 overtime win by the Leafs.

What made the game so bizarre was that a highly contagious influenza bug wreaked havoc on the Senators before and during the game. Wade Redden was forced to sit out with it. Karel Rachunek and Chris Neil (who, incredibly, managed to find the strength to fight Toronto's Nathan Perrott) both had to leave the game because of the 'flu.

The Senators' short bench looked like a revolving door as players were running back and forth between the toilet and the bench. Despite being sick, Hnidy played the entire game and was often seen with his head slumped over on the bench.

"I've never seen anything like it," uttered Senators' defenceman Curtis Leschyshyn. "I saw three guys getting

Battle of Ontario

intravenous. They brought in soup and rice just to try and get food into the guys. I saw players lying on couches with blankets wrapped around them before an NHL game. It's beyond comprehension. All I could do was laugh. It was quite comical."

"Seven or eight guys were sick right before the game," added Bryan Smolinski. "There were pails [around the dressing room]. Some guys were getting sick just off the other guys getting sick."

To make matters worse, the Senators lost Marian Hossa three minutes into the game when he took a puck in the face while killing a penalty, leaving a long smear of blood on the ice. He suffered a severe cut near his right temple.

How did the Leafs feel about their rival's strange predicament? "Boo hoo," cried Owen Nolan after scoring the winning goal. "So what. I don't care. We were tired, too. But we found a way to battle back. I'm sure they've got their excuses ready to go."

It was just another night at the office in the Battle of Ontario.

As the March trading deadline approached, John Muckler once again went shopping for some much-needed toughness. First, he traded for rugged Anaheim defenceman Todd Simpson and re-signed tough guy Rob Ray. Muckler then surprised many by acquiring star forward Peter Bondra from the Washington Capitals. Many critics were not convinced that the high-powered Senators needed another goal scorer, but Muckler argued that you could never have enough for a long playoff run. On deadline day, the Senators also grabbed bruising defenceman Greg de Vries from the Rangers.

Muckler attempted to quell speculation that he was making these deals to get the Senators ready for the Maple Leafs. "We're not building our team to beat the Toronto Maple Leafs. We're building our team to win the Stanley Cup. I would never give Toronto that much credit."

Prior to the final regular season game between the two adversaries, the rivalry took another strange turn when Ottawa city council passed a resolution banning all Maple Leafs jerseys from the final game. Maple Leaf fans in the city were outraged. But in truth, the resolution had a greater purpose. The punishment for those wearing a Leafs jersey was a food donation to the Ottawa food bank.

Heading into the 2004 playoffs, the Leafs were favoured to beat the Senators. At the trade deadline, they had added veterans Brian Leetch, Calle Johansson, and Ron Francis to a line-up that already included stars Mats Sundin, Alex Mogilny, Joe Nieuwendyck, and Owen Nolan. In goal, the Leafs were set with Ed Belfour — provided his nagging back injury didn't return.

The Senators were undeniably a more talented team on paper. They had four solid lines led by Alfredsson, Bondra, Bonk, Hossa, Havlat, Jason Spezza, Bryan Smolinksi, and Mike Fisher. Their power play was the best in the NHL, and

Battle of Ontario

their defence, highlighted by all-star seasons by Wade Redden and Zdeno Chara, was second to none.

The biggest question mark was in goal. After a strong regular and post-season in 2003, Patrick Lalime was a model of inconsistency all through 2004. If he played to his potential, the Senators would be hard to beat; if he didn't, the series would be short and not so sweet.

As the players prepared for the series and showered their rivals with streams of clichéd compliments, the media did their best to stir things up between the fans. For the most part, it was good-natured fun. Someone paid to have a small plane circle Toronto's CN Tower with a banner that said, "LEAFS SUCK." Radio stations in Toronto and Ottawa each composed song parodies of their rival. The Ottawa radio station also printed "Leafs Suck" t-shirts, and held a contest awarding the wildest Senators fan with seats behind the Maple Leafs bench. However, the festivities took a nasty turn when Ottawa radio host Don Romani made some shocking comments about Tie Domi.

While discussing a story about Domi's wife, Romani broadcast, "One would suspect that she could take a good punch."

It was nasty stuff that clearly crossed the line. While Domi refused to discuss the issue, his agent threatened to sue the station. Romani apologized the next day for his comments and was suspended indefinitely by the station.

Toronto Sun columnist Steve Simmons, responding to

the off-ice tomfoolery, summed it up well: It was time to "let the hockey start and the idiocy end."

Heading to Toronto for games one and two, the Senators just wanted to win one to take away the Leafs' home advantage. While the Senators came out flying in the first period, blanketing the Toronto attack with stellar forechecking, it was the Leafs who held a 2-1 lead after the first period.

The Maple Leafs gave the game away in the second by taking a number of unnecessary penalties. In a span of 40 seconds, the Senators took a 3-2 lead.

Hossa clinched the victory with a highlight-reel goal just 1:39 into the third period. Vaclav Varada knocked Johansson off the puck at Toronto's blue line and Hossa raced down the ice after the loose puck. As Belfour charged out of his crease towards the puck, Hossa went flying over Belfour. While in mid-air, Hossa managed to keep his eye on the puck and swept it into the vacated net as he hit the ice.

Ottawa came away with a 4-2 win in game one.

Thanks in large part to the stellar play of Ed Belfour, the Leafs rebounded to take games two and three by 2-0 scores. The Senators, by most accounts, outplayed the Leafs in both games, but spent most of the time making fancy passes along the perimeter rather than sending people towards the net to create traffic in front of Belfour. Without anyone in front of the net, Belfour was able to see shots with relative ease.

Heading into game four, the media wondered if Ottawa would ever score again in the series. When Gary Roberts put

Battle of Ontario

the Leafs up 1-0 at 16:53 in the first, Ottawa fans could be forgiven for experiencing déjà vu. Appropriately, it was Daniel Alfredsson — who assured fans that Ottawa would score in game four — who finally ended Belfour's shutout streak at 157 minutes when he backhanded a Martin Havlat pass by the Toronto goalie.

Ottawa was clearly relieved by the goal. The Senators' play picked up considerably and they cruised to a 4-1 victory to even the series at 2-2.

In one game, the momentum in the Battle of Ontario had swung full circle back into the laps of the Ottawa Senators.

The Senators responded with what might have been their worst playoff performance to date. Though the Leafs only fired 16 shots at Patrick Lalime, a fluke Tie Domi rebound that deflected off Bryan Smolinski was all Toronto needed. Joe Nieuwendyck added a second goal — which Lalime should have stopped — late in the third to give the Leafs a 2-0 victory and a 3-2 series lead.

The loss left Ottawa fans and management frustrated. It wasn't as if the Leafs had outplayed the Senators. Toronto had played a very safe, defensive game that had generated very little in the way of offence. Rather than take advantage of the Leafs' hesitant play, the Senators had stooped to their level. They played without any sense of urgency or fire.

With their backs against the wall and down 1-0 early in the third period of game six, Zdeno Chara scored to even the score at 1-1 and send the game into overtime.

After a scoreless first overtime, Ottawa rookie Antoine Vermette picked up the puck behind the Leafs net early in the second overtime. Fighting off defenceman Aki Berg, Vermette cycled to the front of the net and fired a pass through the crease to a waiting Mike Fisher, who re-directed the puck neatly into the net.

The Senators had crossed one hurdle. Now they had to return to Toronto to cross the biggest stumbling block in franchise history. A victory would conquer a demon and keep their drive for the Stanley Cup alive. A loss would be a serious blow to the credibility of the team and franchise.

Which Senators team would show up into game seven?

The teams exchanged few scoring chances early in the first period, but established a good pace. At 6:43, Toronto struck first for the seventh time in the series. Tie Domi, Toronto's best forward in the series, won a battle with Anton Volchenkov behind the Ottawa boards, and fired a pass to Chad Kilger who shot the puck past Lalime.

Only 1:22 later, Joe Nieuwendyk raced down the left side and fired a harmless looking shot from just inside the blue line. As Lalime went to snare the puck, it dropped and went past him into the net. Less than eight minutes into the most important game in franchise history, the Senators were down 2-0.

With a minute remaining in the period, Greg de Vries was caught out of position and Toronto broke out with an

Battle of Ontario

odd-man rush. Once again, Nieuwendyk headed down the left side of the Senators zone. From an awkward angle, Nieuwendyk fired the puck between the legs of Lalime.

That was all the Leafs needed and they eliminated the Senators with a 4-1 win. For the fourth time in five years, the Toronto Maple Leafs had won the Battle of Ontario and eliminated the Ottawa Senators.

For the Ottawa Senators, the Battle of Ontario raged on.

Epilogue

Following the Senators' first round loss to the Toronto Maple Leafs in the 2004 Stanley Cup playoffs, the mood in Ottawa was understandably grim. After their success in the 2003 playoffs, the Senators were picked by many to win the Stanley Cup in 2004. At the very least, the team was expected to go deep into the post-season.

With a new owner who was willing to increase the team's budget, the relative maturity of the team's young stars, and the late season addition of veterans Peter Bondra, Todd Simpson, and Greg de Vries, everything was in place for the Senators to win it all. But when it mattered most, their best players failed to shine. Alfredsson, Havlat, Redden, Bonk, Bondra, Smolinski, de Vries, and Lalime all performed well below expectations.

Heading into the off-season, major changes were expected. All season long, fans worried about goaltender Patrick Lalime's abilities to lead the Senators. His terrible performance in game seven against the Leafs verified their concerns. Others felt that the team's laissez-faire attitude in big games was a reflection of milquetoast coach Jacques Martin.

One of those concerns was quickly addressed. Two

Epilogue

days after the loss, Martin was fired as coach after eight and a half years.

Despite the uncertainty and gloom surrounding the team following their disappointing 2004 season, there was a lot to like about the future of the Ottawa Senators. The New York Islanders, Edmonton Oilers, Colorado Avalanche, Detroit Red Wings, Dallas Stars, and New Jersey Devils had all stumbled before in their quest for Stanley Cup victories. The Senators had only been an elite NHL team for three seasons and their top players were still young.

Only eight years earlier, the Ottawa Senators — on and off the ice — were the laughing stock of the National Hockey League. In the short time since then, overcoming many off-ice distractions, the Senators had matured into one of the most respected and successful franchises in the NHL.

Bibliography

Diamond, Dan; Duplacey, James; Dinger, Ralph; Fitzsimmons, Ernie; Kuperman, Igor; Zweig, Alan. *Total Hockey: The Official Encyclopedia of the National Hockey League*. Total Sports Publishing, 2000

Finnigan, Joan. *Old Scores, New Goals: The Story of the Ottawa Senators*. Quarry Press, 1992.

Galloway, Bill. "The Glory Years: The Ottawa Senators 1893-1934" printed in *Above the Olympian Hill: Three Hockey Stories*. Jeremiah Lawrence Green, 1993.

Holzman, Morey; Nieforth Joseph. *Dollars and Deceptions*. The Dundurn Group, 2002.

Hunter, Douglas. *Champions: The Illustrated History of Hockey's Greatest Dynasties*. Penguin Studio, 1997.

MacGregor, Roy. *Road Games: A Year in the Life of the NHL*. Macfarlane, Walter & Ross, 1993.

Acknowledgments

I'd like to thank Matthew Firth, Roy Robinson, and Barry Doyle for being good folks. Thanks to Stephen Smith and Altitude for the opportunity. Thanks to Kelly, Betty, and Jarvis Neall for their ongoing support, love, and all that good stuff.

The author also acknowledges various issues of *The Ottawa Citizen*, *The Ottawa Sun*, *The Globe and Mail*, *The National Post*, and *The Toronto Star* for some of the information contained in this book.

Photo Credits

Cover: Dave Sandford/Getty Images; Dave Sandford/Hockey Hall of Fame: pages 60, 79, 96 & 111; Dave Sandford/CHL/Hockey Hall of Fame: page 86; Doug MacLellan/Hockey Hall of Fame: page 49.

About the Author

Chris Robinson lives in Ottawa with his wife and son. He is the artistic director of the Ottawa International Animation Festival and writes a controversial monthly column called *The Animation Pimp* for Animation World Magazine (Los Angeles). His first book, *Between Genius and Utter Illiteracy: A Story of Estonian Animation*, was published in May 2003, and his second manuscript, *Stole This From A Hockey Card: A Philosophy of Doug Harvey, Hockey, Childhood and Booze* is being shopped around. His writing has appeared in Salon.com, Stop Smiling, Mean, 12gauge, Chunklet, The Ottawa Xpress, and a whole slew of international publications. He is currently working on *Hockey on The Rocks: A History of Alcohol and Hockey*, along with a novel *Fathers of Night*.